The Presidents of the United States

❧

The First Twenty Years

❧

Compiled by

John Guidas
and Marilyn K. Parr

Humanities and Social Sciences Division

The Library of Congress
Washington
1993

∞ The paper used in this publication meets the minimum requirements of American National Standard for Information Sciences—Permanence of Paper for Printed Library Materials, ANSI Z39.48–1984.

Library of Congress Cataloging-in-Publication Data

Guidas, John.
    The presidents of the United States : the first twenty years / compiled by John Guidas and Marilyn K. Parr.
        p.   cm.
    Includes indexes.
    ISBN 0–8444–0698–8
    1. United States—Politics and government—1789–1815. 2. Presidents—United States—History—18th century.   3. Presidents—United States—History—19th century.   I. Parr, Marilyn K., 1947– II. Title.
  Z1239.G84 1993
  [E310]
  016.973'099—dc20   92–18145
                                                        CIP

For sale by the U.S. Government Printing Office
Superintendent of Documents, Mail Stop: SSOP, Washington, DC 20402-9328
ISBN 0-16-041610-8

CONTENTS

PREFACE

The following bibliographies will, we hope, inform the researcher as to where he or she might look for information about the lives and administrations of the first three presidents, George Washington, John Adams, and Thomas Jefferson. Our intention was to produce a list of important, useful, and interesting books that will be of service both to the scholar and the generalist. Articles, by and large, were excluded to keep the bibliographies reasonably brief. Extensive bibliographies in many of the works cited will lead the reader seeking further information about specific subjects to specialized articles. The annotations seek to convey the scope of the work cited and to present its author's point of view.

A chapter is devoted to each president in order of succession. Within each of these sections works by the particular president appear first; complete editions of these precede collections of selected works, and separately published works follow. These are all arranged, generally, by date of publication. Works about the president are next. A largely chronological arrangement was chosen for Washington and Adams, in part because we hoped to give some indication of changes in the historical treatment of the subject over the years and in part because the preponderance of books about them are general biographies. We preferred a topical approach for Jefferson because the material seemed to arrange itself best that way. Within these topical headings, works about Jefferson are chronologically arranged to reflect the changes in historiography.

The last bibliography of the presidents issued by the Library, *The Presidents of the United States, 1789–1962: A Selected List of References* (Washington, Library of Congress, 1962), was the starting point for the present work, and in a few cases we have retained its annotations or notes.

Those looking for further information about Washington, Adams, or Jefferson and those seeking information about other presidents may wish to consult Ronald M. Gephart's *Revolutionary America, 1763–1789* (Washington, Library of Congress, 1984), *The American Presidency* (Santa Barbara, Calif., ABC-Clio Information Services, 1984), Fred I. Greenstein's *Evolution of the Modern Presidency: A Bibliographical Survey* (Washington, American Enterprise Institute for Public Policy Research, 1977), Fenton S. Martin's *American Presidents: A Bibliography* (Washington, Congressional Quarterly Inc., 1987), and Norman S. Cohen's *The American Presidents: An Annotated Bibliography* (Pasadena, Calif., Salem Press, 1989).

The compilers received encouragement and assistance from Marguerite Bloxom, Larry Boyer, Edward P. Cambio, Marvin Kranz, Barbara Morland, and R. David Myers. Thanks are extended to them all.

INTRODUCTION

The inauguration of George Washington on April 30, 1789, marked the beginning both of his administration and of the presidency itself. The framers of the Constitution had delivered a blueprint. They provided in Article II the sturdy beams needed to support a strong and independent executive. The actual construction was left for the craftsmen who would erect the structure. George Washington, John Adams, and Thomas Jefferson would have the task of making this new office, the presidency, at least habitable. Succeeding presidents would complete the edifice, making alterations and renovations as required by their times, but much of the presidency we recognize today, especially our ideas of presidential conduct and our concepts of the powers and duties of the office, is attributable to these first three presidents.

FIGURE 1. View of the Inauguration of Washington as Seen from Broad Street. (LC–USZ62–21297)

The Presidents
of the
United States

The First Twenty Years

FIGURE 2. Martha Washington in Her Early Days, From the Original by Alonzo Chappel. Johnson Fry & Co., Philadelphia. (LC–USZ62–11649)

Chapter I

George Washington

Compiled by John Guidas

WRITINGS OF GEORGE WASHINGTON

Collected Writings

1

The Writings of George Washington from the original manuscript sources, 1745–1799 ; prepared under the direction of the United States George Washington Bicentennial Commission and published by authority of Congress / John C. Fitzpatrick, editor. — Washington : U.S. Govt. Print. Off., [1931–44]. — 39 v. : ill., fronts. (incl. ports.), maps (1 fold.), plans, facsims. (part fold.).

E312.7 1931

Reprinted in Westport, Conn. by Greenwood Press in 1970. Washington's "essential" writings, including many of his letters and general orders, but not his diary. For over fifty years this has been the standard edition of Washington's papers. Jared Sparks's *The Writings of George Washington* (Boston, American Stationers' Co., 1834–1837) is neither complete nor textually accurate, and Worthington C. Ford's *The Writings of George Washington* (New York, Putnam, 1889–1893) omits many items.

2

Calendar of the correspondence of George Washington, commander in chief of the Continental army, with the Continental Congress / prepared from the original manuscripts in the Library of Congress by John C. Fitzpatrick, Division of Manuscripts. — Washington : U.S. Govt. Print. Off., 1906. — 741 p. : front., facsims. — (Washington papers ; I)

Z6616.W3 U47

3

Index to the George Washington papers. — Washington : [U.S. Govt. Print. Off.], 1964. — xxxi, 294 p. — (Presidents' papers index series)

Z8950 .U64

Includes an introductory essay by Dorothy S. Eaton on the provenance of the papers. A slightly revised version of this essay appeared in the *Quarterly Journal of the Library of Congress*, Vol. 22, (Jan. 1965) ; p. 3–26.

4

The Papers of George Washington. Colonial series / W.W. Abbot, editor ; Dorothy Twohig, associate editor ; Philander D. Chase, Beverly H. Runge, and Frederick Hall Schmidt, assistant editors. — Charlottesville : University Press of Virginia, 1983– <1988 >. — v. <1–6 > : ill.

E312.72 1983

Includes bibliography and indexes.
Contents: 1. 1748–August 1755 — 2. August 1755–April 1756 — 3. April–November 1756 — 4. November 1756–October 1757 — 5. October 1757–September 1758 — 6. September 1758–December 1760 —

This edition, when completed, with its companions, *The Papers of George Washington. Revolutionary War Series* and *The Papers of George Washington. Presidential Series*, will replace Fitzpatrick's work (item no. 1) as the standard collection of Washington's writings. The editors have endeavored to reproduce the texts of the documents accurately and have published, when available, the letters of Washington's correspondents.

5

The Papers of George Washington. Revolutionary War series / Philander D. Chase, editor. — Charlottesville : University Press of Virginia, 1985– <1988 >. — v. <1–2 >.

E312.72 1985

Contents: 1. June–September 1775 — 2. September–December 1775 — January–March 1776 —

6

The Papers of George Washington. Presidential series / Dorothy Twohig, editor. — Charlottesville : University Press of Virginia, 1987– <1989 >. — v. <1–2 >.

E312.72 1987b

Contents: 1. September 1788–March 1789 — 2. April–June 1789 —

7

The Diaries of George Washington / Donald Jackson, editor ; Dorothy Twohig, associate editor. — Charlottesville : University Press of Virginia, 1976–1979. — 6 v. : ill.

E312.8 1976

Includes bibliographies and indexes.

The diaries cover most of Washington's adult life, although there are significant gaps during the Revolutionary War years and during his presidency. Washington was a matter-of-fact diarist; he generally recorded events without reflecting on their meanings or revealing much about his feelings. Extensive annotations inform the reader about the people, places, and events mentioned. John C. Fitzpatrick's *Diaries, 1748–1799* (Published for the Mount Vernon Ladies' Association of the Union, Boston, Houghton Mifflin, 1925) is substantially the same in text but his annotations are much briefer.

Selected Writings

8

Maxims of Washington : political, social, moral, and religious / collected and arranged by John Frederick Schroeder. — New York : D. Appleton, 1855. — xxiv, [13]–423 p.

E312.79 .W3124

Frequently reprinted, most recently in Mount Vernon, Va., by the Mount Vernon Ladies' Association of the Union in 1988.

A selection of Washington quotations arranged by subject. Citations to the sources and an index are included.

9

Basic writings of George Washington / ed., with an introduction and notes, by Saxe Commins. — New York : Random House, [1948]. — xvii, 697 p.

E312.72 1948

Selections are arranged chronologically to show Washington's role in the great events of his times. Brief editorial notes explain the background or significance of the documents.

10

The Washington papers : basic selections from the public and private writings of George Washington / edited and arr., with an introd., by Saul K. Padover. — [1st ed.]. — New York : Harper, [1955]. — 430 p.

E312.72 1955

Bibliography: p. 417–418.

These excerpts were selected to reveal his personality and character.

11

Affectionately yours, George Washington : a self-portrait in letters of friendship / edited by Thomas J. Fleming. — New York : Norton, [1967]. — 280 p.

E312.74 1967

Washington is often thought of as an aloof man with a chilly personality. This selection of his personal letters is intended to demonstrate his essential warmth and friendliness.

12

George Washington : a biography in his own words / edited by Ralph K. Andrist ; with an introd. by Donald Jackson ; Joan Paterson Kerr, picture editor. — New York : Newsweek ; distributed by Harper & Row, [c1972]. — 416 p. : ill. — (The Founding Fathers)

E312 .W33 1972

Bibliography: p. 408.

Although Washington refused to write an autobiography, his other writings are substantial and varied enough to allow one to reconstruct his life in his own words. Editorial notes link and explain the selections. The book is based on Donald Jackson's edition of *The Papers of George Washington*.

13

George Washington : a collection / compiled and edited by W.B. Allen. — Indianapolis : Liberty Classics, c1988. — xxvii, 714 p. : ill.

E312.72 1988

Taken mostly from Fitzpatrick's edition of Washington's writings. Brief essays link the selections.

Individual Works

14

The Journal of Major George Washington : sent by the Hon. Robert Dinwiddie, esq., His Majesty's lieutenant-governor, and commander in chief of Virginia, to the commandant of the French forces on Ohio. To which are added the Governor's letter: and a translation of the French officer's answer. With a new map of the country as far as the Mississippi — Williamsburgh printed; London : Reprinted for T. Jefferys, 1754. — 32 p. : front. (fold. map).

E312.8 1754 Rare Bk. Coll.

Covers the period from October 1753 to January 1754.

A facsimile of the first printing was issued in Williamsburg, Va., by Colonial Williamsburg and distributed by Holt in 1959.

In 1753 Washington, a major of the Virginia militia, delivered a message of warning to the French at Fort Le Boeuf, who were disputing British control of the Ohio country. Upon his return, Governor Dinwiddie had Washington's journal printed to alert Virginia to the danger presented by the French. The journal was subsequently published in London as well.

15

Letters from His Excellency George Washington : president of the United States of America, to Sir John Sinclair, bart., M.P., on agricultural, and other interesting topics. Engraved from the original letters, so as to be an exact facsimile of the handwriting of that celebrated character. — London : Printed by W. Bulmer and co., and sold by G. and W. Nicol, 1800. — 57 p. incl. facsims.

E312.75 .A24

Includes facsimiles of eight letters, dated from October 20, 1792, to November 6, 1797.

Sinclair, a proponent of scientific agriculture and first president of the Board of Agriculture, had sent Washington some recently published papers on that subject. Washington's reply in these letters is indicative of his interest in the improvement of breeds and crops, in methods of cultivation, and in the general promotion of agriculture. Washington's letters to Arthur Young, a colleague of Sinclair and secretary to the same board, were also published as *Letters from General Washington to Arthur Young Containing an Account of His Husbandry* (London, W. J. and J. Richardson, 1801). Both sets of letters were later republished in Franklin Knight's *Letters on Agriculture from His Excellency George Washington, President of the United States* (Washington, The editor, 1847).

16

Correspondence of the American Revolution : being letters of eminent men to George Washington, from the time of his taking command of the army to the end of his presidency / ed. from the original manuscripts by Jared Sparks. — Boston : Little, Brown, 1853. — 4 v.

E203 .S73

Reprinted in Freeport, N.Y., by Books for Libraries Press in 1970.

This was for many years the principal published source for letters to Washington, and will be so until the University Press of Virginia's edition of *The Papers of George Washington* is finished. Readers should be aware of Sparks's readiness to alter or eliminate passages he thought inappropriate. See Stanislaus Murray Hamilton's *Letters to Washington* (item no. 19) for another selection of correspondence received by Washington.

17

The Washington-Crawford letters : being the correspondence between George Washington and William Crawford, from 1767 to 1781, concerning western lands. With an appendix, containing later letters of Washington on the same subject; and letters from Valentine Crawford to Washington, written in 1774 and 1775, chronologically arranged and carefully annotated / by C. W. Butterfield. — Cincinnati : R. Clarke, 1877. — xi, 107 p.

E312.75 .O37

Crawford, a Virginian, had moved into southwestern Pennsylvania, an area then also claimed by Virginia. Washington learned that the Pennsylvania authorities were prepared to sell land in the area and wrote to Crawford, whom he had known in Virginia, asking him to act as Washington's agent in acquiring good land in the region. The correspondence is illustrative of Washington's interest in western land and of his methods of acquiring it.

18

Washington-Irvine correspondence : the official letters which passed between Washington and Brig.-Gen. William Irvine and between Irvine and others concerning military affairs in the West from 1781 to 1783. Arranged and annotated, with an introduction containing an outline of events occurring previously in the Trans-Alleghany country / by C. W. Butterfield. — Madison, Wis. : D. Atwood, 1882. — vi p., 1 leaf, 430 p. : front., ports., fold. map.

E203 .B98

General Irvine was headquartered at Fort Pitt and was charged with the defense of the northwestern frontier in the later part of the Revolutionary War.

19

Letters to Washington, and accompanying papers [1752–July 1, 1775]. published by the Society of the Colonial Dames of America / ed. by Stanislaus Murray Hamilton. — Boston and New York : Houghton Mifflin, 1898–1902. — 5 v. : 2 facsim. (incl. front.)

E312.2 .H22

Until the University Press of Virginia's *The Papers of George Washington* is completed this and Jared Sparks's *Correspondence of the American Revolution* will continue to be the major published sources for letters sent to Washington.

20

George Washington's accounts of expenses while commander in chief of the Continental army, 1775–1783 / reproduced in facsimile, with annotations by John C. Fitzpatrick. — Boston and New York : Houghton Mifflin, 1917. — vii, 154, 1 leaf : front., facsims. (port.)

E312.81 1917

"The accounts of the expenses of the commander in chief of the Continental army were kept in duplicate by Washington himself. One he transmitted, at the close of the war, to the Board of Treasury of the Continental Congress for auditing . . . the other he retained, and it is from this document, now in the Library of Congress, that the accounts are now reproduced in photographic facsimile"—Pref. note.

21

The Agricultural papers of George Washington / ed. by Walter Edwin Brooke. — Boston : R.G. Badger, [c1919]. — xviii p., 1 leaf, 17–145 p.

E312.75 .A2

Selected letters and extracts from his diaries, farm reports, and other papers which demonstrate that he was a skilled and scientific agriculturist.

FIGURE 3. Descending the Ohio. (LC–USZ62–42846)

22

Washington's farewell address : in facsimile with transliterations of all the drafts of Washington, Madison, & Hamilton, together with their correspondence and other supporting documents / edited, with a history of its origin, reception by the nation, rise of the controversy respecting its authorship, and a bibliography, by Victor Hugo Paltsits. — New York : New York Public Library, 1935. — xvi, 102 p., 1 leaf, facsim. (p. 105–136), 1 leaf, 139–360 p., 1 leaf : front. (col. port.), facsims.

E312.95 1935 Rare Bk. Coll.

"Bibliography of the Farewell Address": p. [305]–360.

23

George Washington's Rules of civility and decent behaviour in company and conversation / edited with an introduction by Charles Moors; with frontispiece and facsimiles. — Boston & New York : Printed for Houghton Mifflin Co. by the Riverside Press, Cambridge, 1926. — xiv, 64 p. : ill., front., (port.), facsims.

E312.78 1926

"Comparison between the Washington Rules of civility and Hawkins's 'Youths behaviour' " : p. [23]–[65].

Reprinted in Williamsburg, Va., by Beaver Press in 1971 with a cover title: George Washington's book of etiquette.

Found among Washington's school exercises, these have appeared in many editions since 1886. Moors traces the origin of the maxims to a French Jesuit treatise of 1595 via Francis Hawkins's *Youths Behaviour*, a popular English work of the seventeenth century.

24

Washington, sa correspondance avec d'Estaing. — Paris : Publié par les soins de la Fondation nationale pour la reproduction des manuscrits précieux et pièces rares d'archives, [1937]. — 2 p. leaves, iv, 65 p., 1 leaf : ill., fold. facsims.

E312.74 1937

Letters exchanged between Washington and the Comte d'Estaing, commander of the French fleet. D'Estaing's letters are accompanied by English translations.

25

General Washington's correspondence concerning the Society of the Cincinnati / edited by Lieutenant Colonel Edgar Erskine Hume. — Baltimore : The Johns Hopkins Press, 1941. — xliv, 472, [3] p. : front. (port.), facsims. (1 fold.).

E312.75 .S6

Includes a brief history of the society and reprints some documents significant in its history.

26

The Letters of Lafayette to Washington, 1777–1799 / edited by Louis Gottschalk. — 2nd printing / edited and revised by Louis Gottschalk and Shirley A. Bill. — Philadelphia : American Philosophical Society, 1976. — xlii, 433 p. — (Memoirs of the American Philosophical Society ; v. 115)

Q11 .P612 v. 115

Includes bibliographical references and indexes.

Supersedes first printing privately issued in New York in 1944.

27

George Washington, 1732–1799 : chronology, documents, bibliographical aids / edited by Howard F. Bremer. — Dobbs Ferry, N.Y. : Oceana Publications, 1967. — 90 p. — ([Oceana presidential chronology series ; 1])

E312 .B8

Bibliography: p. 81–87.

28

The Journal of the proceedings of the president, 1793–1797 / Dorothy Twohig, editor. — Charlottesville : University Press of Virginia, 1981. — xvii, 393 p., [1] leaf of plates : ill.

E312.8 1793–1797

Bibliography: p. xiii–xvii.

An executive daybook, kept by Washington's secretaries, it records much of the daily business of his administration and is particularly valuable because his personal diaries for much of the period covered have been lost. Entries for later years are sparse.

29

A Fairfax friendship : the complete correspondence between George Washington and Bryan Fairfax, 1754–1799 / edited by Donald M. Sweig and Elizabeth S. David ; prepared for, and under the direction of, the Fairfax County History Commission by the History and Archaeology Section of the Office of Comprehensive Planning, Fairfax County, Virginia. — Fairfax County, Va. : The Commission, 1982. — xi, 170 p., [1] leaf of plates : ill.

E312.74 1982

Includes bibliographical references.

A portrait of Washington as a friend, neighbor, and advisor to the younger Fairfax.

BIOGRAPHIES AND OTHER STUDIES

(Entries are arranged chronologically by date of publication.)

30
Marshall, John.
    The life of George Washington : commander in chief of the American forces during the war which established the independence of his country, and first president of the United States / compiled under the inspection of the Honourable Bushrod Washington, from original papers . . . to which is prefixed an introduction, containing a compendious view of the colonies planted by the English on the continent of North America, from their first settlement to the commencement of that war which terminated in their independence by John Marshall. — Philadelphia : Printed and published by C.P. Wayne, 1804–07. — 5 v. : front. (port.)

                E312 .M33 Rare Bk. Coll.

    Frequently reprinted, abridged, etc. The most recent edition in LC was published in New York by AMS Press in 1969 (E312. M364).

    Published by subscription, and much delayed, the first volumes were poorly received because they comprised a general history of the colonies from Columbus to the beginnings of the Revolution, compiled from older works and having little of Washington in them. The demands of his publishers compelled Marshall to compress the later volumes, resulting in a tightly written history of Washington's role in the Revolution and of his presidency, sharpened by Marshall's own knowledge of or participation in many of the events recounted. Though Marshall knew Washington, he rarely offers personal insight into Washington's character and limits himself to the man's public career. Marshall's Federalist bias is clear, though subtly expressed.

31
Gibbs, George.
    Memoirs of the administrations of Washington and John Adams : edited from the papers of Oliver Wolcott, secretary of the treasury / by George Gibbs. — New York : Printed for the subscribers [W. Van Norden, printer], 1846. — 2 v. : front. (port.)

                E311 .G44

    Reprinted in New York by B. Franklin in 1971.

    Wolcott rose through several important posts in the Treasury Department to become secretary in 1795 after Hamilton's resignation. He remained there through the rest of Washington's administration and continued under Adams until the end of 1800. The extracts from his correspondence published here and linked by Gibbs's historical passages are illustrative of the policies and politics of the administrations in which he served.

32
Irving, Washington.
    Life of George Washington / by Washington Irving. — New York : G. P. Putnam, 1855–1859. — 5 v. : ill., plates, 7 port. (incl. fronts.), 12 maps (3 double), double facsim.

                E312 .I6

    Frequently reprinted, abridged, etc. The most recent edition in LC was reprinted in New York by AMS Press in 1973.

    Irving's novelistic style creates a livelier Washington, more the cavalier hero, than is depicted in Marshall's stately lines, but neither goes beyond a narration of his public career.

33
Custis, George Washington Parke.
    Memoirs of Washington / by his adopted son, George Washington Parke Custis, with a memoir of the author by his daughter, and illustrative and explanatory notes by Benson J. Lossing. — [Philadelphia] : Edgewood Pub. Co., [1859]. — 644 p. : front. (port.)

                E312.15 .C957 Rare Bk. Coll.

    Other editions published 1859, 1860, and 1861 under title: *Recollections and Private Memoirs of Washington*.

    Stresses Washington's home and family life. The work is considered unreliable by many authorities because of its dependence upon hearsay and its incorporation of popular but unfounded myths.

34
Baker, William Spohn.
    Character portraits of Washington as delineated by historians, orators and divines / selected and arranged in chronological order, with biographical notes and references, by W.S. Baker. — Philadelphia : R.M. Lindsay, 1887. — 351 p. : front.

                E312.17 .B16

    Selections range from first-hand observations by his contemporaries to late nineteenth-century orations. Eulogies are not included.

35
Ford, Worthington Chauncey.
    Washington as an employer and importer of labor / [edited by Worthington Chauncey Ford]. — Brooklyn, N.Y. : priv. print., 1889. — v, 6–78 p.

                E312.17 .F69

    Reprinted in New York by B. Franklin in 1971.

    Contents: Introductory note [signed Worthington Chauncey Ford] — Contracts, agreements, etc. — Importing Palatines, 1774 — Advertisement of runaway servants — Form of indenture or covenant for servants.

FIGURE 4. Washington as a Farmer. (LC–USZ62–39290)

36

Baker, William Spohn.

Itinerary of General Washington from June 15, 1775, to December 23, 1783 / by William S. Baker. — Philadelphia : Lippincott, 1892. — 2 p. leaves, 334 p. : ill., front. (port.)

E312.27 .B16

Reprinted, with additions, from the *Pennsylvania Magazine of History and Biography*, v. 14–15.

Washington's activities and whereabouts day by day from his appointment as commander in chief to his farewell to Congress.

37

Ford, Paul Leicester.

The true George Washington / by Paul Leicester Ford. — Philadelphia : Lippincott, 1896. — 319 p. : ill., 5 plates, 8 port. (incl. front.), 2 maps, 9 facsim.

E312 .F6

Reprinted in Freeport, N.Y., by Books for Libraries Press in 1971 (E312 .F719 1971).

Not a biography but a series of topical essays in which Ford, a popular novelist of the time, looks at Washington, his family, social life, farming, and amusements.

38

Baker, William Spohn.

Washington after the Revolution, MDCCLXXXIV–MDCCXCIX / by William Spohn Baker. — Philadelphia : J.B. Lippincott, 1898. — 2 p. leaves, [3]–416 p.

E312.39 .B14

A sequel to Baker's *Itinerary of General Washington*, this book records Washington's daily activities from the end of the Revolutionary War to his death.

39

Lodge, Henry Cabot.

George Washington / by Henry Cabot Lodge. — Rev. ed. — Boston and New York : Houghton Mifflin, 1898. — 2 v. : ill., fronts., plates, ports., fold. facsim.

E312 .L82

Frequently reprinted, most recently in New York by AMS Press in 1972. Lodge's fame derives from his long career in the Senate, but he was also a professionally trained historian. This biography is intended to reveal "the unknown man," but it concentrates largely on his public life.

40

Ford, Paul Leicester.

Washington and the theatre / by Paul Leicester Ford. — New York : Dunlap Society, 1899. — 5 p. leaves, 68 p., 1 leaf, 14 p. : ill., front., plates, facsims.

E312.17 .F67
PN2016 .D7 new ser. no. 8

On cover: Publications of the Dunlap Society. New Series, no. 8.

Reprinted in New York by B. Franklin in 1970.

Playgoing was a popular recreation among Virginia's gentry, and one for which Washington developed a taste while young. Ford describes the early theater in America and relates incidents of Washington's attendance at various plays.

41

Wister, Owen.

The seven ages of Washington : a biography / by Owen Wister. — New York : Macmillan, 1907. — xv, 263 p. : front., 4 plates, 4 port.

E312 .W8

Laments the mythologizing of Washington, the pious image of him that prevailed in nineteenth century biographies, and draws a series of loose prose portraits of him at various stages of life.

42

Fielding, Mantle.

Gilbert Stuart's portraits of George Washington / by Mantle Fielding. — Philadelphia : Printed for the subscribers, 1923. — xii, 264 p. : front., ports.

E312.43 .F54

Extensive introductory and biographical material about artist and subject precedes a catalog of 124 of the portraits.

43

Henderson, Archibald.

Washington's southern tour, 1791 / by Archibald Henderson. — Boston and New York : Houghton Mifflin, 1923. — xxvii, 339, [1] p. : ill., front., plates, ports., facsims.

E312.27 .H47

As president, Washington made tours of the northern, eastern, and southern states to show himself to the people and to engender support for the new central government. This detailed account includes descriptions of the physical, social, and cultural settings in which Washington and his party found themselves.

44

Haworth, Paul Leland.

George Washington, country gentleman : being an account of his home life and agricultural activities / by Paul Leland Haworth . . . with many illustrations, facsimiles of private papers, and a map of Washington's estate drawn by himself. — Indianapolis : Bobbs-Merrill, [c1925]. — 7 p. leaves, 336 p. : ill., front., plates, facsims.

E312.17 .H392

Published in 1915 under title: George Washington, farmer.

Describes the daily operations at Mt. Vernon, including crops and livestock, Washington's management practices, the use of servants and slaves, and family life and recreations.

45

Hughes, Rupert.

George Washington / [by] Rupert Hughes. — New York : W. Morrow, 1926–1930. — 3 v. : fronts., ill. (incl. maps, plans), ports., facsims.

E312 .H924

"Books Consulted and Quoted": v. 1, p. 565–572; v. 2, p. 675–683; v. 3, p. 796–810.

Contents: [v. 1] The Human being and the hero, 1732–1762 — [v. 2] The Rebel and the patriot, 1762–1777 — [v. 3] The Savior of the states, 1777–1781.

Attempts to clear away the legends and myths which surround Washington. Its critical approach and its reexamination of old scandals brought it much controversy, though Hughes concludes there is more to admire in Washington's character than not.

46
Woodward, William E.
George Washington : the image and the man / by W.E. Woodward. — New York : Boni & Liveright, 1926. — 5 p. leaves, 9–460 p., xiii–xxxv p. : front., ports., plan, facsim. Bibliography: p. xiii–xxvi.

E312 .W896

A not always favorable interpretation of Washington's character and personality. This is, with Hughes's work above, one of the so-called "debunking" biographies popular after the First World War.

47
Fitzpatrick, John Clement.
George Washington, colonial traveller, 1732–1775 / by John C. Fitzpatrick . . . with a map by the author. — Indianapolis : Bobbs-Merrill, [c1927]. — xiv p., 2 leaves, 416 p. : ill., incl. front. (map).

E312.27 .W3

Records Washington's day-to-day activities and whereabouts, insofar as they can be determined from his diaries and other papers. The work completes William S. Baker's *Itinerary of General Washington from June 15, 1775, to December 23, 1783* and his *Washington after the Revolution, 1784–1799.*

48
Prussing, Eugene E. (Eugene Ernst)
The estate of George Washington, deceased / by Eugene E. Prussing. — Boston : Little, Brown, 1927. — xii p., 512 p. : front., plates, ports., maps (part fold.), facsims.

E312.5 .P98

Discusses the circumstances of Washington's death, his descendants and legatees, and the disposition of his holdings in considerable detail. Appendices reprint Martha Washington's will, an inventory of the contents of Mount Vernon, and other relevant documents about Washington's estate.

49
Fay, Bernard.
George Washington, republican aristocrat. — Boston : Houghton Mifflin, 1931. — xvi p., 297 p. : front., ports., maps.

E312 .F32

"Sources and Notes": p. [275]–286.
By birth and upbringing a "feudal lord," Washington, through his heroic deeds and the force of his character, became the exemplar of classic republican virtue.

50
Morgan, John Hill.
The life portraits of Washington and their replicas / by John Hill Morgan and Mantle Fielding. — Philadelphia. Printed for the subscribers ; [Lancaster, Pa. : Lancaster Press, c1931]. — xxiii, 432 p. : ill., col. front., plates, ports.

E312.43 .M85
N7628.W3 M6

Includes biographies of the artists.

51
Van Dyke, Paul.
George Washington : the son of his country, 1732–1775 / by Paul Van Dyke. — New York : Scribner, 1931. — 5 p. leaves, 310 p. : ill., front. (port.), facsim.

E312.2 .V24

"References": p. [293]–301.
Washington was partly a product of his environment, but he possessed talents and abilities that distinguished him from and enabled him to rise above other political or military leaders with similar backgrounds.

52
Eisen, Gustav.
Portraits of Washington / [by] Gustavus A. Eisen. — New York : R. Hamilton & associates, 1932. — 3 v. : ill., front. (v. 1–2, col.), plates, ports., facsims.

E312.43 .E37 Rare Bk. Coll.

Bibliography: v. 3, p. 969–989.
Contents: — Portraits in oil painted by Gilbert Stuart / by G.A. Eisen assisted by C.J. Dearden — Portraits in oil painted by Charles Willson Peale and others; also miniatures, crayons, charcoal and line drawings by James Sharples, C.B.J.F. de Saint Memin, and others / by G.A. Eisen— Sculptured portraits, including statues, busts, reliefs, and masks, in wax, marble, and plaster / by G.A. Eisen ; assisted by W.S. Conrow.

53
Helderman, Leonard Clinton.
George Washington : patron of learning / by Leonard C. Helderman. — New York : Century Co., [c1932]. — xv, 187 p. : ill., front. (port.), plates, facsims.

E312.17 .H48

Discusses the state of education in Washington's time, his advocacy of a national university, and his connections to Washington and Lee University, the United States Military Academy, Washington College, and Alexandria Academy.

54
Knox, Dudley Wright.
The naval genius of George Washington / by Dudley W. Knox . . . with a foreword by Admiral Hilary P. Jones. — Boston : Houghton Mifflin, 1932. — 6 p. leaves, 3–137 p. : ill., front., plates, ports., maps.

E312.25 .K67

"List of Sources": p. [129]–[132].
Though not a naval commander, nor even much acquainted with the arts of naval warfare, Washington understood fully the importance of sea power to victory.

FIGURE 5. Washington's Sketch for a Cipher and Crest for His Coach.

55

Morison, Samuel Eliot.

The young man Washington / by Samuel Eliot Morison. — Cambridge : Harvard University Press, 1932. — 43 p.

E132.17 .M86

This essay was reprinted in the author's *By Land and By Sea: Essays and Addresses* (New York, Knopf, 1953) without the notes included here.

A remembrance of the youthful Washington learning, working, and playing will serve as a counterweight to his image of somewhat stuffy remoteness.

56

Sears, Louis Martin.

George Washington / by Louis Martin Sears. — New York : Thomas Y. Crowell, [c1932]. — xiv, 560 p. : ill., front. (port.), maps.

E312 .S44

"Bibliographical note": p. 523–525.

The tendency to emphasize the human failings of great men, seen in several of the Washington biographies written in the 1920s, leads readers to ignore the qualities that produced greatness says Sears, intending to right the balance with this work. He portrays Washington as a man marked by character, abilities, and destiny for leadership (but not necessarily sainthood). His magnanimity enabled him to surmount the squabbling pettiness which marked the careers of many of his peers while his insight into human nature supplied him the shrewdness to deal with the egos of those around him.

57

Tatsch, Jacob Hugo.

The facts about George Washington as a freemason / by Major J. Hugo Tatsch. — 3rd ed. — New York : Macoy Publishing and Masonic Supply Co., 1932. — xvi p., 1 leaf, 100 p. : ill., front., plates, port.

E312.17 .T294

"A List of Masonic Books about George Washington": p. 89. "Other Books on Washington": p. 90–91.

58

George Washington Bicentennial Commission (U.S.)

History of the George Washington bicentennial celebration. Literature series. — Washington : United States George Washington Bicentennial Commission, 1932. — 3 v. : ill., col. fronts., (some col. ports., maps, plans, facsims.), col. fold. plate.

E312.6 .U58

Vols. 1–2 contain bibliographies.

The Bicentennial Commission published a great deal of Washingtoniana. Some of the pamphlets, essays, and factual compilations collected and published here may still provide useful bits of information difficult to locate elsewhere.

59

Decatur, Stephen.

Private affairs of George Washington from the records and accounts of Tobias Lear, esquire, his secretary / by Stephen Decatur, Jr. — Boston : Houghton Mifflin, 1933. — xv, 1 leaf, 356 p. : ill., front., ports., facsims.

E312.29 .D32

Bibliography: p. 335–[337].

Reprinted in New York by Da Capo Press in 1969.

Based on the household account books kept by Lear during Washington's first term, to which Decatur has added much explanatory material taken from original letters, diaries, and contemporary newspapers.

60

Fitzpatrick, John Clement.

George Washington himself : a common-sense biography written from his manuscripts / by J. C. Fitzpatrick. — Indianapolis : Bobbs-Merrill, [c1933]. — xiii p., 17–544 p. : ill., front. (port.).

E312 .F52

Reprinted in Westport, Conn., by Greenwood Press in 1975.

Sticking closely to the story as told in Washington's own writings, Fitzpatrick defends him against contemporary rivals and twentieth-century critics.

61

Whittemore, Frances Dean Davis.

George Washington in sculpture / by Frances Davis Whittemore. — Boston : Marshall Jones, 1933. — xv, 203 p., xlvii plates (incl. front.) on 16 leaves.

E312.4 .W47

Describes various statues, busts, medals, and other memorials to Washington located almost entirely in the United States. The work does not have footnotes and lacks an index.

62

De La Bedoyere, Michael.

George Washington : an English judgment / by Michael De La Bedoyere. — London : Harrap, [1935]. — 309 [1] p. : ill., front., maps, plates, ports., facsim.

E312 .D45

Bibliography: p. 301–304.

A brief interpretive biography written to make "the real Washington" better known to British readers.

63

Ambler, Charles Henry.

George Washington and the West / by Charles H. Ambler. — Chapel Hill : University of North Carolina Press, 1936. — viii, 270 p. : ill., maps, plates, 2 port. (incl. front.).

E312 .A62

"Select Bibliography": p. 249–259.

Reprinted in New York by Russell & Russell in 1971.

Washington's military career on the frontier and his interest in acquiring property there are a foreshadowing of the future importance of the region to the United States.

FIGURE 6. Washington and Liberty.

64

Chinard, Gilbert.

George Washington as the French knew him : a collection of texts / edited and translated, with an introduction, by Gilbert Chinard. — Princeton : Princeton University Press, 1940. — xviii, 161 p. : ill., plate, 2 port. (incl. front.)

E312.17 .C5

Reprinted in New York by Greenwood Press in 1969.

The texts include descriptions or impressions of Washington gathered from the writings of French officers, travelers, and notables such as Talleyrand, Guizot, and de Tocqueville.

65

Knollenberg, Bernhard.

Washington and the Revolution, a reappraisal : Gates, Conway, and the Continental Congress / by Bernhard Knollenberg. — New York : Macmillan, 1940. — xvi p., 1 leaf, 269 p. : front. (port.).

E312.25 .K64

"Table of Books Cited": p. 232–250.

"Manuscript Collections Cited": p. 251.

Reprinted in Hamden, Conn. by Archon Books in 1968.

Washington, contrary to the opinions of Fitzpatrick and other biographers, was not solely responsible for the success of the Revolution, though, if one accepted Washington's own writings uncritically, it might appear as if he were. Washington was determined to present himself always as in the right and had a knack for putting the blame for his mistakes onto others. Consequently, the Continental Congress and other political and military leaders deserve a larger share of the credit for the political and military success of the Revolution than they have usually been accorded.

66

Stephenson, Nathaniel W. (Nathaniel Wright)

George Washington / by Nathaniel Wright Stephenson and Waldo Hilary Dunn. — New York ; London : Oxford University Press, 1940. — 2 v. : ill., fronts., plates, ports., maps, facsims.

E312 .S82

"Bibliographical Note": p. 403–404.

Bibliographical references included in "Notes" v. 1, p. 405–473; v. 2, p. 505–566.

After the death of Dr. Stephenson, the incomplete work was revised and the last seven chapters written by Waldo Hilary Dunn.

67

Leduc, Gilbert Francis.

Washington and "the murder of Jumonville" / by Gilbert F. Leduc ; published under the auspices of La Société Historique Franco-américaine. Boston : [s.n.], 1943. — 2 p., iii p., 3 leaves, [17]–235 p., 2 leaves : ill., maps, facsims., front. (port.).

E312.23 .L43

Bibliography: p. [229]–235.

In 1754 Washington was sent at the head of an expeditionary force to reconnoiter French activity in the Ohio country and to warn the French away from British-claimed territory. His force encountered and attacked a French encampment. Among those killed was Joseph Coulon, Sieur de Jumonville. Jumonville carried diplomatic credentials, which Washington did not know about. His death caused an uproar. Washington was accused of murdering a diplomat. Leduc defends Washington against these charges, maintaining that Jumonville was acting as a spy rather than an ambassador.

68

Freeman, Douglas Southall.

George Washington : a biography. — New York : Scribner, 1948–[1957]. — 7 v. : ill., ports., maps, facsims.

E312 .F82

Includes bibliographies.

Reprinted in Clifton, N.J., by A.M. Kelley in 1975. Several abridgments have also appeared.

Contents: v. 1–2. Young Washington — v. 3. Planter and patriot — v. 4. Leader of the revolution — v. 5. Victory with the help of France — v. 6. Patriot and president — v. 7. First in peace / by John Alexander Carroll and Mary Wells Ashworth.

A massive and highly detailed classic.

69

Bellamy, Francis Rufus.

The private life of George Washington. — New York : Crowell, [1951]. — v, 409 p.

E312 .B45

Bibliography: p. 387–401.

Attempts to uncover the very private person at the center of public life.

70

Nettels, Curtis P. (Curtis Putnam)

George Washington and American independence. — [1st ed.]. — Boston : Little, Brown, 1951. — 338 p. : ports., maps.

E312.25 .N4

Bibliography: p. [313]–324.

Reprinted in Westport, Conn., by Greenwood Press in 1976.

Describes the events in England and America which led the Second Continental Congress to name Washington as commander in chief and portrays him as the principal actor in the move to have the Congress declare for independence.

71

Bryan, William Alfred.

George Washington in American literature, 1775–1865. — New York : Columbia University Press, 1952. — xii, 280 p. : ports.

PS169.W3 B7

Bibliography: p. [247]–269.

Reprinted in Westport, Conn., by Greenwood Press in 1970.

Description and criticism of portrayals of Washington in biography, oratory, poetry, drama, and fiction.

72

Swiggett, Howard.

The great man : George Washington as a human being. — [1st ed.]. — Garden City, N.Y. : Doubleday, 1953. — 491 p.

E312 .S9

Bibliography: p. [465]–469.

Defends Washington against criticisms from his contemporaries and from historians and other commentators. Swiggett portrays him as one who consistently did "the right thing" because to do otherwise would have been to accept personal defeat.

73

Tebbel, John William.

George Washington's America. — [1st ed.]. — New York : Dutton, 1954. — 478 p. : fold. map.

E312.27 .T4

"Reference Notes": p. 452–460.

A relation of Washington's everyday life against the background of the country and the people he knew or saw in the course of his personal travels, his military campaigns, and his presidential tours. Tebbel describes how the country looked to him and how he looked to his contemporaries.

74

Cleland, Hugh.

George Washington in the Ohio Valley. — Pittsburgh : University of Pittsburgh Press, 1955. — xiii, 405 p. : ill., plates, ports., maps, facsims. — ([Western Pennsylvania series])

E312 .C62

Bibliographical footnotes.

The early history of the upper Ohio Valley as it affected Washington and was itself changed by his interest in it and his travels there.

75

Wright, Esmond.

Washington and the American Revolution. — London : English Universities Press, [1957]. — 192 p. — (Teach yourself history library)

E312.25 .W73

A brief survey of Washington's life and contributions by a British historian.

76

Cunliffe, Marcus.

George Washington, man and monument. — Boston : Little, Brown, [1958]. — 234 p. : ill.

E312 .C88

"Further Reading": p. [217]–223.

Washington the man became in his own lifetime Washington the myth, a chilly marble idol who might have inspired Emerson's "Every hero becomes a bore at last." Cunliffe describes Washington's career and the mythologizing process and in them uncovers qualities shared by the person and the legendary figure.

77

Sears, Louis Martin.

George Washington & the French Revolution. — Detroit : Wayne State University Press, 1960. — x, 378 p.

E312.29 .S4

Bibliography: p. 355–359.

Reprinted in Westport, Conn., by Greenwood Press in 1973.

Washington's correspondence with Americans in France and with his personal friends among the French is the basis for Sears's interpretation of Washington's response to the events of the Revolution. Personally sympathetic to the Revolution's goals, Washington's overriding concern for American interests led him to adopt an official policy of cool neutrality.

78

Bemis, Samuel Flagg.

George Washington and Lafayette, the prisoner in Europe. — In his American foreign policy and the blessings of liberty and other essays / by Samuel Flagg Bemis. — New Haven : Yale University Press, 1962. — p. 209–239.

E183.7 .B44

Originally published in the *Daughters of the American Revolution Magazine*, v. 58, June–Aug. 1924: p. 341–350, 407–414, 481–489.

Reprinted in Westport, Conn., by Greenwood Press in 1975.

After fleeing the Terror in revolutionary Paris, Lafayette was imprisoned by the allies. He appealed to the United States for assistance, but the cautious efforts of its diplomats were unsuccessful. Washington's personal representations on his behalf were equally unavailing. Lafayette's freedom was finally secured after a peace was arranged between France and the European powers.

79

Boller, Paul F.

George Washington & religion. — Dallas : Southern Methodist University Press, [1963]. — 235 p.

E312.17 .B74

"Selected Bibliography": p. 219–227.

Taking his evidence from Washington's own writings rather than from the abundant anecdotal material that exists on the subject, Boller concludes that Washington was "broadly speaking" a Deist, but one who customarily observed most of the practices of the Anglican Church and who viewed organized religion as a stabilizing force in society.

80

Knollenberg, Bernhard.

George Washington : the Virginia period, 1732–1775. — Durham, N. C. : Duke University Press, 1964. — x, 238 p.

E312.2 .K56

Bibliography: p. [197]–210.

Topical discussions of his early life, including his service in the French and Indian War, his relationships with family members, his work in local and parish government, and his involvement with the Revolution up to his election as commander in chief. Knollenberg bases his account solely on contemporary evidence and critically examines Washington's own statements.

FIGURE 7. Portrait of Washington by Rembrandt Peale, Original in U.S. Capitol. (LC–USA7–525)

81

Flexner, James Thomas.

George Washington. — Boston : Little, Brown, [1965–1972]. — 4 v. : ill., facsims., maps, ports.

Includes bibliographies.

Contents: v. 1. George Washington : the forge of experience, 1732–1775 [E312.2 .F6] — v. 2. George Washington in the American Revolution, 1775–1783 [E312.25 .F69] — v. 3. George Washington and the New Nation, 1783–1793 [E312.29 .F55] — v. 4. George Washington : anguish and farewell, (1793–1799 [E312.29 .F56]).

Flexner admires the man Washington made of himself; he learned from his mistakes, overcame his limitations, and developed his talents and abilities. Though not without fault and foible, Washington gradually became the towering figure who, more than any other, was responsible for the successful outcome of the Revolutionary War and for the creation of a new government that would be able to sustain itself.

Flexner's later one-volume biography, *Washington, the Indispensable Man* (Boston, Little, Brown, 1974. E312 .F556) stresses the same themes.

82

Kinnaird, Clark.

George Washington : the pictorial biography. — [1st ed.]. — New York : Hastings House, [1967]. — vi, 265 p. : ill., facsims., maps, plans, ports.

E312 .K56

Bibliography: p. 255–256.

Contains reproductions of numerous eighteenth and nineteenth-century paintings and other illustrative matter purporting to show Washington and the world he knew.

83

Borden, Morton.

George Washington / [compiled by Morton Borden]. — Englewood Cliffs, N.J. : Prentice-Hall, [1969]. — vi, 154 p. — (Great lives observed ; A Spectrum book)

E312 .B6

Bibliographical footnotes.

Excerpts from Washington's own writings, from those of his contemporaries, and from an array of biographers and historians aimed at providing a brief but balanced assessment of his character and achievements.

84

Kaufman, Burton Ira.

Washington's farewell address : the view from the 20th century. — Chicago : Quadrangle Books, 1969. — 192 p.

E312.952 .K3

Includes text of Washington's Farewell Address.

Includes bibliographical references.

The address has become a part of the national consciousness and has been used by both isolationists and interventionists in support of their policy aims. Included with the speech are a number of contemporary assessments and interpretations of the address and of its influence on American foreign policy.

85

Mellon, Matthew Taylor.

Early American views on Negro slavery : from the letters and papers of the founders of the Republic / [by] Matthew T. Mellon. — [New ed.] with a new introd. by Richard B. Morris. — New York : Bergman Publishers, [1969]. — xvii, 187 p.

E446 .M47 1969

"The views considered are those of Benjamin Franklin and the first four presidents of the United States."

Bibliography: p. 179–182.

Growing up amid the brutalities of slavery, Washington came gradually to abhor it. His experiences in the Revolutionary War and elsewhere had broadened his mind and made his attitude toward African Americans more humane. He could not bring himself to manumit his own slaves whether out of fear of alienating other slave holders or for personal economic reasons, though he did provide for their gradual freedom in his will.

86

Smith, James Morton.

George Washington : a profile / [compiled by James Morton Smith]. — [1st ed.]. — New York : Hill and Wang, [1969]. — xxx, 289 p. — (American profiles)

E312 .S64

Bibliography: p. 286–289.

Collection of essays and excerpts reflecting Washington historiography from 1932 to 1968.

87

Callahan, North.

George Washington, soldier and man. — New York : Morrow, 1972. — xiii, 296 p. : ill.

E312.25 .C28

Bibliography: p. [281]–284.

Washington's military career concisely recounted. Callahan sees him as the general who led the colonies to independence and whose love of liberty and greatness of character secured constitutional government for the new nation.

88

Ketchum, Richard M.

The world of George Washington / by Richard M. Ketchum. — New York : American Heritage Pub. Co. ; book trade distribution by McGraw-Hill, [1974]. — 275 p. : ill.

E312 .K47 1974

Heavily illustrated to convey, as realistically as possible, an image of the country, people, and material universe that Washington knew.

Copyright, 1876, by Currier & Ives, N.Y.

ALEXANDER HAMILTON, Secy. of the Treasury.

GEN.ᴸ HENRY KNOX, Secy. of War.

THOMAS JEFFERSON, Secy. of State.

GEORGE WASHINGTON.

EDMUND RANDOLPH, Attorney General.

WASHINGTON AND HIS CABINET.

NEW YORK PUBLISHED BY CURRIER & IVES, 125 NASSAU ST.

FIGURE 8. Washington and His Cabinet, Lithograph by Currier and Ives. (LC–USZ62–1306)

89

McDonald, Forrest.
  The presidency of George Washington. — Lawrence :
University Press of Kansas, [1974]. — xi, 210 p. : port.
— (American presidency series)
                                              E311 .M12
Bibliography: p. 187–199.
  Washington had mixed success as a president in achiev-
ing political goals. His real contribution to the office and to
the nation rose out of his character and what he came to
symbolize rather than from specific policies. A quarrelsome
people fractured on political and sectional lines neverthe-
less unanimously elected him president. His dignity and
probity infused the office with a stature and charisma
which his successors would draw on in order to govern.
The Constitution may have created the presidency, but
Washington gave the office the authority it still retains.

90

Davis, Burke.
  George Washington and the American Revolution /
Burke Davis. — 1st ed. — New York : Random House,
c1975. — 497 p. : maps.
                                           E312.25 .D38
Bibliography: p. [461]–464.
  Colorful history of Washington's military operations em-
phasizing the personalities of those involved and the hard-
ships they endured.

91

Emery, Noemie.
  Washington : a biography / Noemie Emery. — New York :
Putnam, c1976. — 432 p.
                                          E312 .E43 1976
Bibliography: p. 415–421.
  Finds the key to his character in the formative events of his
childhood and youth. The early death of his father and his
mother's excessive concern for his safety made him cautious
and somewhat aloof, but also gave him self-reliance, a desire for
adventure, and a sense of his personal freedom. The death of
his brother, Lawrence, brought him property and position and
a heightened sense of responsibility; he assumed leadership of
his family and took on Lawrence's unfulfilled ambitions.

92

Morgan, Edmund Sears.
  The meaning of independence : John Adams, George
Washington, Thomas Jefferson / by Edmund S. Morgan. —
Charlottesville : University Press of Virginia, 1976. — 85 p.
: ports. — (Richard lectures for 1975, University of Virginia)
                                           E322 .M85
Includes bibliographical references and index.
  Washington's character was typified by some traits that
do not usually appear in a good revolutionary. He was icily
aloof, remote, kept a steady eye on his own economic interests, and put great value on honor and appearance. In the
course of the Revolution these served him well. He came to
see that nations as well as individual men are motivated
jointly by honor and self-interest. Honor alone will not
keep an army in the field; the pay must be adequate.

93

Morgan, Edmund Sears.
  The genius of George Washington / Edmund S. Morgan. — Washington : Society of the Cincinnati, 1980. —
91 p., [2] leaves of plates : ports. — (George Rogers
Clark lecture ; 3, 1977)
                                          E312.63 .M839
Includes bibliographical references and index.
  Washington, otherwise not especially gifted, understood
the nature of power, whether political or military, and knew
how to exercise it better than some of his brilliant contemporaries, such as Hamilton and Jefferson. Because of this, he
was able first to secure independence for America and then
to establish its domestic government and foreign relations
on a solid basis. A selection of Washington's letters which illustrate Morgan's thesis is appended.

94

Wall, Charles Cecil.
  George Washington, citizen-soldier / Charles Cecil
Wall. — Charlottesville : University Press of Virginia,
1980. — xiv, 217 p. : ill.
                                              E312 .W29
Bibliography: p. 205–207.
  Reprinted in Mount Vernon, Va., by the Mount Vernon
Ladies' Association in 1988.
  Uses unpublished domestic records of Mount Vernon
and letters Washington wrote to his family and friends at
home to illustrate his continuing concern and involvement
with his beloved plantation in the midst of war.

95

Aikman, Lonnelle.
  Rider with destiny : George Washington / by Lonnelle
Aikman. — 1st ed. — McLean, Va. : Link Press, 1983. —
vii, 173 p. : ill. (some col.)
                                          E312 .A54 1983
Bibliography: p. 163–166.
  Heavily illustrated depiction of Washington at Mount Vernon
and of his involvement in the planning of Washington, D.C.

96

Reuter, Frank T. (Frank Theodore)
  Trials and triumphs : George Washington's foreign pol-
icy / by Frank T. Reuter. — 1st ed. — Fort Worth : Texas
Christian University Press, c1983. — xxiii, 249 p. : ill. —
(A.M. Pate, Jr. series on the American presidency ; v. 2)
                                          E311 .R385 1983
Bibliography: p. [232]–243.
  Surveys world politics at the beginnings of Washington's
presidency and details his administration's dealings with
Britain, France, and Spain, the major powers most inter-
ested in North American affairs.

97
Alden, John Richard.
  George Washington : a biography / John R. Alden. —
  Baton Rouge : Louisiana State University Press, c1984.
  — xii, 326 p., [13] p. of plates : ill., ports. — (Southern
  biography series)
                                        E312 .A58 1984
  Bibliography: p. 307–315.
  Scholarly synthesis of current interpretations of Wash-
  ington's life, with emphasis on his military career.

98
Wills, Garry.
  Cincinnatus : George Washington and the Enlightenment.
  — 1st ed. — Garden City, N.Y. : Doubleday, 1984. — xxvi,
  272 p., [4] p. of plates : ill.
                                        E312.62 .W54 1984
  Bibliography: p. 245–258.
  A newly born America needed its creation myths and he-
  roes as symbols of unity. Artists and writers enhanced Washington's charisma by portraying his deeds and character as
  those of a secularized god. Wills brings the methods of art
  history to this study of the mythicizing of Washington.

99
Higginbotham, Don.
  **George Washington and the American military tradi-
  tion** / Don Higginbotham. — Athens : University of
  Georgia Press, c1985. — xii, 170 p. : port. — (Mercer
  University, Lamar memorial lectures ; no. 27)
                                        E312.17 .H63 1985
  Bibliography: p. [139]–161.
  Traces the development of Washington's thought on civil
  control of the military and related issues. As a young officer
  on the western frontier he sought military rank and glory
  and condemned the civil authorities who were not forthcom-
  ing with supplies and troops when needed. In his middle
  years when he served in the House of Burgesses and the
  Continental Congress he came to value the processes of de-
  liberative government and to see the dangers of a military establishment beyond the control of civil authority. As commander in chief he was mediator between the army and the
  Congress, pleading the case of the former but defending the
  latter when its authority was challenged.

100
Jones, Robert Francis.
  George Washington / Robert F. Jones. — Rev. ed. —
  New York : Fordham University Press, 1986. — 180 p.
                                        E312 .J79 1986
  Bibliography: p. 172–176.
  Stresses Washington's extraordinary self-discipline and
  devotion to duty as the elements of his character which en-
  abled him to surmount otherwise average abilities and tal-
  ents and to become a symbol of unity for the colonies and
  then for the nation.

101
Schwartz, Barry.
  George Washington : the making of an American symbol / Barry Schwartz. — New York : Free Press ; London
  : Collier Macmillan, c1987. — xii, 250 p., [24] p. of
  plates : ill., ports.
                                        E312 .S39 1987
  Bibliography: p. 209–242.
  Analyzes the processes by which Washington became a
  "totem," a personification of the values of American society,
  whose real and ascribed virtues remain the standard against
  which, consciously or not, Americans measure their leaders.

102
Ferling, John E.
  The first of men : a life of George Washington / John E.
  Ferling. — 1st ed. — Knoxville : University of Tennessee
  Press, c1988. — xiii, 598 p. : ill.
                                        E312 .F47 1988
  Bibliography: p. [579]–584.
  Primary source material is augmented by recent research
  on Washington and the Revolutionary era to produce a por-
  trait of Washington that balances his continuing interest in
  his business and agricultural ventures, his family life, and
  his involvement in public affairs.

103
Longmore, Paul K.
  The invention of George Washington / Paul K. Longmore. — Berkeley : University of California Press, c1988.
  — x, 337 p.
                                        E312.17 .L84 1988
  Bibliography: p. 305–317.
  From his youth Washington understood what was
  needed to achieve high status in his society: substantial
  property, an imposing style of life, the proper dress and
  manners, dignified carriage, position in public life, freedom
  from dependence on others, and military success. He consciously shaped his public image to these requirements almost as an actor would adapt himself to a stage role. His re-
  strained interpretation of "The Great Man" role convinced
  others of his rightness for the part.

  An appended essay argues that Washington was, contrary
  to the opinion of most of his biographers, quite well read in
  history, literature, and politics as well as in agriculture and
  the practical arts.

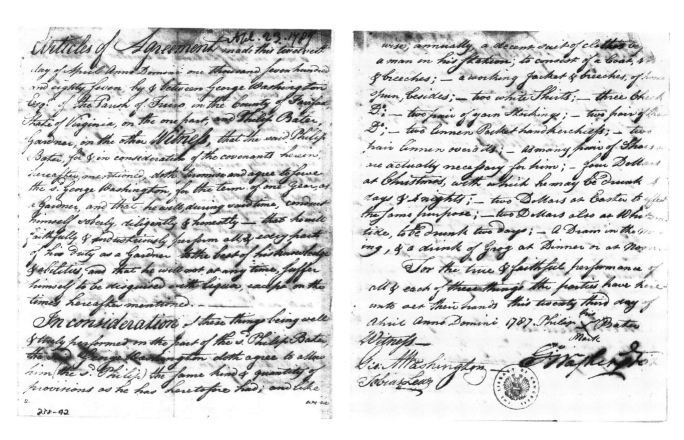

FIGURE 9.   Contract between Washington and His Gardener, 1787,
Original in George Washington Papers, Manuscript Division, Library of Congress.

104

Marling, Karal Ann.

George Washington slept here : colonial revivals and American culture, 1876–1986 / Karal Ann Marling. — Cambridge, Mass. : Harvard University Press, 1988. — xii, 453 p. : ill.

E312.17 .M3 1988

Bibliography: p. 393–439.

The Philadelphia Centennial Exhibition of 1876 saw the beginnings of the colonial revival. Georgian or federal architecture began to replace Queen Anne and other nineteenth-century styles. Silhouettes of George and Martha appeared on the walls of middle-class homes; "Martha Washington sewing cabinets" were sold in every department store; some old myths about Washington, such as his "vision" at Valley Forge, were given new circulation. The suggestion of early American dignity and rectitude transmitted by these symbols, and especially by anything associated with Washington, was used to convey a variety of positive self-images to Americans dissatisfied with the directions that industrialization and urbanization were taking the country. Washington became, on the one hand, the embodiment of traditional values and virtues, while on the other his persona was infused with the contemporary concerns of successive generations.

105

A Great and good man : George Washington in the eyes of his contemporaries / edited by John P. Kaminski and Jill Adair McCaughan ; sponsored by the Center for the Study of the American Constitution, the New York Commission on the Bicentennial of the United States Constitution [and] the Virginia Commission on the Bicentennial of the United States Constitution. — Madison, Wis. : Madison House, 1989. — xi, 244 p.

E312.62 .G63 1989

The esteem and affection Americans of the Revolutionary generation felt for Washington is illustrated by this selection of correspondence, addresses, excerpts from newspapers, and poems.

FAMILY, HOMES, AND HAUNTS

106

Moors, Charles.

The family life of George Washington / by Charles Moors ; with an introduction by Mrs. Theodore Roosevelt. — Boston and New York : Houghton Mifflin, 1926. — xvi p., 1 leaf, 250 p. : ill., front., plates, ports., maps (1 double), facsims.

E312 .M75

A discussion of his ancestry with biographical sketches of several members of his family.

107

Duke, Jane Taylor.

Kenmore and the Lewises / [by Jane Taylor Duke] ; foreword by Harry Flood Byrd. — [1st ed.]. — Garden City, N.Y. : Doubleday, 1949. — xvi, 268 p. : ill., ports.

E312.19 .D84

"Notes (bibliographical)": p. [233]–257.

Relates the story of Elizabeth, Washington's only sister, and her husband, Colonel Fielding Lewis. The Lewises built a fine home, Kenmore, just outside of Fredericksburg, Virginia, where Washington was often a guest. The latter part of the work describes the preservation and restoration of the estate, which is now open to the public.

108

Stetson, Charles Wyllys.

Washington and his neighbors. — Richmond : Garrett and Massie, [1956]. — xii, 342 p. : ill., ports., map (on lining papers)

E312.17 .S82

Bibliography: p. 314–319.

Washington the family man, planter, neighbor, and country gentleman, depicted at Mount Vernon, in the nearby town of Alexandria, and in the northern Virginia countryside.

109

Thane, Elswyth.

Washington's lady. — New York : Dodd, Mead, 1960. — 368 p. : ill.

E312.19.W95 T48

"A Bibliographical Note": p. 353–356.

Unlike Abigail Adams, Eleanor Roosevelt, or other first ladies who left a substantial body of their writings behind them, very little remains from the pen of Mrs. Washington, which makes it difficult to see her personality and activities clearly. She destroyed almost all the correspondence between herself and her husband after his death. Thane's account is based on remarks about her in Washington's other letters and on other contemporary sources.

110

Thane, Elswyth.

Mount Vernon is ours : the story of its preservation. — [1st ed.]. — New York : Duell, Sloan and Pearce, [1966]. — viii, 467 p. : maps, ports.

E312.5 .T5

Bibliography: p. 453–454.

111

Carroll, Frances Laverne.

The library at Mount Vernon / by Frances Laverne Carroll and Mary Meacham. — Pittsburgh, Pa. : Beta Phi Mu, c1977. — 184 p. : ill. — (Beta Phi Mu chapbook ; no. 12)

Z997.W32 C36

Bibliography: p. [174]–180.

FIGURE 10. Washington's Commission as Commander in Chief of the Army, Original in George Washington Papers, Manuscript Division, Library of Congress. (LCMSS–044693–40)

112
Muir, Dorothy Troth.
General Washington's headquarters, 1775–1783. — Troy, Ala. : Troy State University Press, c1977. — xv, 79 p. : ill.

E312.27 .M84

Bibliography: p. 77–79.

113
Bourne, Miriam Anne.
First family : George Washington and his intimate relations / Miriam Anne Bourne. — 1st ed. — New York : Norton, c1982. — 212 p., [10] p. of plates : ill.

E312.19 .B68 1982

Bibliography: p. 211–212.

Washington as paterfamilias, leading the country in war and peace but simultaneously involved with and deeply concerned about his large family and its sometimes bewildering problems.

114
Torres, Louis.
"To the immortal name and memory of George Washington" : the United States Army Corps of Engineers and the construction of the Washington Monument / by Louis Torres. — Washington : Historical Division, Office of Administrative Services, Office of the Chief of Engineers : U.S. Govt. Print. Off., 1985. — vii, 145 p., [1] leaf of plates : ill.

F203.4.W3 T67 1985

Bibliography: p. 133–139.

FIGURE 11. John Adams, President of the United States, Etching, Printed and Sold by Amos Doolittle, August 14, 1799. (LC–USZ62–1798)

Chapter II

John Adams

Compiled by John Guidas

WRITINGS OF JOHN ADAMS

(Entries are arranged chronologically by date of publication.)

Collected Writings

115

Microfilms of the Adams papers / owned by the Adams Manuscript Trust and deposited in the Massachusetts Historical Society. — Boston : Massachusetts Historical Society, 1954–

Microfilm Mss

"The papers, public and private, of President John Adams (1735–1826), President John Quincy Adams (1767–1848), and Charles Francis Adams (1807–1886), together with papers of their wives and children." Includes the items not selected for publication in *The Adams Papers.*

116

Adams family correspondence / Lyman H. Butterfield, editor ; Wendell D. Garrett, associate editor ; Marjorie E. Sprague, assistant editor. — Cambridge : Belknap Press of Harvard University Press, 1963– <1973 >. — v. <1–4 > — (The Adams papers ; Series II)

E322.1 .A27

Includes bibliographical references.

Contents: v. 1. December 1761–May 1776 — v. 2. June 1776–March 1778 — v. 3. April 1778–September 1780 — v. 4. October 1780–September 1782 —

117

The Works of John Adams, second president of the United States : with a life of the author, notes, and illustrations / by his grandson Charles Francis Adams. — Boston : Little, Brown, 1850–1856. — 10 v. : fronts. (v. 1–2, 5, 7–10), plates, ports., facsims. (part fold.).

E302 .A26

Contents: v. 1. Life of John Adams / [by C. F. Adams] — v. 2. Diary, with passages from an autobiography. Notes of debates in the Continental Congress, in 1775 and 1776. Autobiography — v. 3. Autobiography (cont.) Diary. Notes of a debate in the Senate of the United States. Essays — v. 4. Novanglus, or A history of the dispute with America, from its origin in 1754 to the present time. Letter to Richard Henry Lee, 15 November 1775. Thoughts on government, applicable to the present state of the American colonies. Letter to John Penn, January 1776. Report of a constitution or form of government for the commonwealth of Massachusetts, 1779. Defence of the constitutions of government of the United States of America, v. 1 — v. 5. Defence of the constitutions, v. 2–3 — v. 6. Defence of the constitutions, v. 3, (cont.). Discourses on Davila. Four letters, being an interesting correspondence between John Adams and Samuel Adams, on government. Three letters to Roger Sherman on the Constitution of the United States. Roger Sherman, to John Adams, in reply. Letters to John Taylor, of Caroline, Virginia, in reply to his strictures on some parts of the Defence of the American constitutions. Review of the propositions for amending the Constitution, submitted . . . in 1808 — v. 7–8. Official letters, messages, and public papers, 1777–1799 — v. 9. Official letters, messages, and public papers, 1797–1801. Correspondence originally published in the Boston *Patriot.* General correspondence, 1770–1811 — v. 10. General correspondence, 1770–1811. Indexes.

The *Life of John Adams* by Charles Francis Adams, v. 1 of this collection, has been published separately and frequently reprinted.

Reprinted in New York by AMS Press in 1971 ; also published in microform in Ann Arbor, Mich., by University Microfilms in 1956–1976 (American culture series ; 269:1, 270:1).

Charles Francis Adams's editorial work was considered excellent by the standards of his time, but his selections from the correspondence and the diary are not as textually reliable as *The Adams Papers.* This collection is a source for some of Adams's longer works which may be difficult to find elsewhere.

118

Papers of John Adams / Robert J. Taylor, editor ; Mary-Jo Kline, associate editor ; Gregg L. Lint, assistant editor. — Cambridge, Mass. : Belknap Press of Harvard University Press, 1977–<1983 >. — v. <3, 5–6 >. : ill. — (The Adams papers ; Series III: General correspondence and other papers of the Adams statesmen)

E302 .A26 1977

Includes bibliographical references and index.

A broad selection of correspondence with nonfamily members, the shorter political writings, and miscellaneous materials.

119

Diary and autobiography / Lyman H. Butterfield, editor, Leonard C. Faber and Wendell D. Garrett, assistant editors. — Cambridge : Belknap Press of Harvard University Press, 1961. — 4 v. : ill., facsims., maps, ports. — (The Adams papers ; Series I: Diaries)

E322 .A3

Contents: v. 1. Diary, 1755–1770 — v. 2. Diary, 1771–1781 — v. 3. Diary, 1782–1804. Autobiography to October 1776 — v. 4. Autobiography, 1777–1780.

Adams recorded his life as a farmer, lawyer, politician, husband, father and friend, resident of a Massachusetts village, and participant in great events, in his diary entries. More than most of his famous contemporaries who kept personal journals, he let his diary reflect his emotions and personality and his impressions of others. The result is a portrait of his character and temperament as well as of his life and times.

120

Legal papers of John Adams / L. Kinvin Wroth and Hiller B. Zobel, editors. — Cambridge, Mass. : Belknap Press of Harvard University Press, 1965. — 3 v. : ill., facsims., map, plan, ports. — (The Adams papers ; Series III: General correspondence and other papers of the Adams statesmen)

LAW

Bibliographical footnotes.

Adams's own notes, together with material from other primary sources, on sixty-four cases representative of his private legal practice, including the two Boston Massacre cases. An introduction and notes explain eighteenth-century legal practice and place the cases in the context of their times.

121

The Earliest diary of John Adams : June 1753–April 1754, September 1758–January 1759 / Lyman H. Butterfield, editor, Wendell D. Garrett and Marc Friedlaender, associate editors. — Cambridge, Mass. : Belknap Press of Harvard University Press, 1966. — xx, 120 p. : ill., ports. — (The Adams papers ; Series I: Diaries)

E322 .A34

"Diary and Autobiography of John Adams, supplement."

Found in the Royall Tyler Collection at the Vermont Historical Society some four years after the publication of the *Diary and Autobiography*, this early collection of diary entries, class notes, miscellaneous observations, and legal notes sheds light on Adams's early years at Harvard, his year as schoolmaster at Worcester, and his early legal career.

122

The Selected writings of John and John Quincy Adams / edited and with an introd. by Adrienne Koch and William Peden. — New York : Knopf, 1946. — 3 p. leaves, xxxix (i.e. 41), 413, xxix p., 1 leaf : 2 port. (incl. front.)

E302 .A28

"Bibliographical note: John Adams": p. 219–221.

"Bibliographical note: John Quincy Adams": p. 411–413.

These selections of previously published materials illustrate the political thought of both Adamses.

123

The Political writings of John Adams : representative selections / edited with an introd. by George A. Peek, Jr. — New York : Liberal Arts Press, [1954]. — 223 p. — (The American heritage series ; no. 8)

JC176 .A3

Few Americans in public life have made the attempt, as Adams did in his writings, to construct a complete and logical system of government, delineated here in brief.

124

The John Adams papers / selected, edited, and interpreted by Frank Donovan. — New York : Dodd, Mead, [1965]. — 335 p. : facsim., ports. — (The Papers of the founding fathers)

E302 .A275

Short excerpts from Adams's diary, letters, and other papers, connected by the editor's comments and explanations, and arranged to cover the successive stages of his career, from lawyer to respected elder statesman.

Individual Works

125

A Defence of the constitutions of government of the United States of America / by John Adams. — London : Printed for C. Dilly, 1787. — 2 v.

JK171 .A2 1787 Rare Bk. Coll.

Reprinted in New York by Da Capo in 1971.

Adams took a leading role in the writing of the Massachusetts Constitution of 1780, a generally conservative document which adapted many of the features of the British constitution to American conditions, as did the constitutions of many of the other states. By the mid 1780s these constitutions were being criticized from abroad by those who believed that the centralized, monarchical governments of the continental powers provided a sounder and more efficient administration and from within the United States by those who wanted a greater measure of democracy. Civil disorder in some states, particularly Massachusetts, which was struggling with Shays's Rebellion, gave the debate urgency. In defense of the Constitution of Massachusetts and of similar constitutions of other states, Adams hastily put together this work, which argues that a stable and just government should incorporate monarchic, aristocratic, and democratic principles and should apportion power among the executive, legislative, and judicial functions through a system of checks and balances.

The edition of this item which appears in *The Works of John Adams* was extensively revised by Charles Francis Adams. He corrected printing errors and transpositions of pages and changed the format from that of a series of letters to one of chapters organized around particular subjects.

126

Discourses on Davila : a series of papers on political history, written in the year 1790 and then published in the Gazette of the United States / by an American citizen. — Boston : Printed by Russell and Cutler, 1805. — 248 p.

JK171 .A23 Rare Bk. Coll.

Reprinted in New York by Da Capo in 1973.

Enrico Caterino Davila fought as a mercenary in the French civil wars of the sixteenth century and later wrote a history of the period which went through a number of editions. Adams used the work as the basis for this series of essays in which he drew parallels between the chaos of that period and the current turmoil in revolutionary France. His prescription was for a government of divided powers, balanced among conflicting elements of society, and drawing its inspiration from a realistic rather than idealistic view of human nature.

127

Correspondence of the late President Adams : originally published in the Boston Patriot. — Boston : Everett and Munroe, 1809[–10]. — iv, 572 p.

E322 .A515 Rare Bk. Coll.

Adams began this series of letters written from April 10, 1809 to February 10, 1810, in a Boston newspaper to justify his position on impressment and on relations with France during his presidency, but went on to review much of his career.

128

Novanglus, and Massachusettensis : or, political essays, published in the years 1774 and 1775, on the principal points of controversy between Great Britain and her colonies / the former by John Adams . . . the latter by Jonathan Sewall . . . to which are added a number of letters, lately written by President Adams to the Honourable William Tudor, some of which were never before published. — Boston : printed and published by Hews & Goss, 1819. — 2 p. leaves, [iii]–vii, [9]–312 p.

E211 .A195 Rare Bk. Coll.

Reprinted in New York by Russell & Russell in 1968. Also published in part as *The American Colonial Crisis, the Daniel Leonard-John Adams Letters to the Press, 1774–1775* in New York by Harper & Row in 1972. The Novanglus letters were also published in an abridged form in London in 1784 under the title *History of the Dispute with America, from Its Origin in 1754.*

In December 1774, a series of letters signed Massachusettensis defending the British position in the dispute with America began to appear in a Boston newspaper. Adams believed the letters were written by Jonathan Sewall, though they are now recognized to be the work of Daniel Leonard. Adams replied in a series of letters signed Novanglus. The earlier letters are a history of the dispute and an indictment of Crown officials, the later a defense of the theory that Parliament had no authority over America. William Tudor was the founder and first editor of the *North American Review.* In these letters Adams reviewed the early years of the controversy with Great Britain, and particularly the role of James Otis in the controversy.

129

Correspondence between the Hon. John Adams : . . . and the late Wm. Cunningham, Esq., beginning in 1803, and ending in 1812. — Boston : E. M. Cunningham, 1823. — x, 219, [1] p.

E310 .A21

Library of Congress copy bound with A Review of the Correspondence by Timothy Pickering (2nd ed., Salem, Cushing and Appleton, 1824).

Shortly after leaving the presidency, Adams began this exchange of letters with Cunningham in which he expressed freely and frankly his often unflattering opinions of the politics and characters of other public figures, such as Hamilton and Jefferson. The correspondence was to have remained unpublished, but, after Cunningham's suicide in 1823, his son, a partisan of Andrew Jackson, published it with the intent of embarrassing Jackson's rival for the presidency, John Quincy Adams.

130

Familiar letters of John Adams and his wife Abigail Adams, during the Revolution : with a memoir of Mrs. Adams / by Charles Francis Adams. — New York : Hurd and Houghton, 1876. — xxxii, 424 p. : front. (port.).

E322 .A518

Reprinted in Freeport, N.Y. by Books for Libraries Press in 1970.

The collection includes only about half the letters exchanged by the Adamses during the Revolution and published in the *Adams Family Correspondence.* The letters were corrected by C.F. Adams to remove errors in spelling or grammar and subjects he thought inappropriate or indecorous.

131

Massachusetts Historical Society.

Warren-Adams letters : being chiefly a correspondence among John Adams, Samuel Adams, and James Warren . . . 1743–1814. — [Boston] : Massachusetts Historical Society, 1917–25. — 2 v. : fronts., plates, port., facsims. — (Massachusetts Historical Society. Collections ; v. 72–73)

F61 .M41 vol. 72–73

Reprinted in New York by AMS Press in 1972.

Letters exchanged among a circle of friends active in colonial, Revolutionary, and national affairs. Although the letters are primarily political in nature, some personal matters are also discussed.

FIGURE 12.   President John Adams, From the Painting by
John Singleton Copley.   (LC–USZ62–1909)

132

Statesman and friend : correspondence of John Adams with Benjamin Waterhouse, 1784–1822 / edited by Worthington Chauncey Ford. — Boston : Little, Brown, 1927. — vi, 178 p.

E322 .A519

The young Waterhouse had lived with Adams in 1778 while he was studying medicine at the University of Leyden and Adams was minister to The Hague. When Waterhouse returned to America to teach and practice medicine he and Adams began to correspond about such topics of mutual interest as natural history, literature, and politics. The letters here are primarily from Adams, Waterhouse's having largely been lost.

133

The Adams-Jefferson letters : the complete correspondence between Thomas Jefferson and Abigail and John Adams / edited by Lester J. Cappon. — Chapel Hill : Published for the Institute of Early American History and Culture at Williamsburg, Va., by the University of North Carolina Press, [1959]. — 2 v. (li, 838 p.) : ill., ports.

E322 .A516

Adams and Jefferson met at the Continental Congress in 1775 where a friendship arose between them. When their duties separated them they began a correspondence which they continued until service in Washington's administration brought them together in New York. Political differences caused them to grow apart in the 1790s and it was not until after Jefferson completed his two terms as president that a reconciliation was effected, largely through the efforts of Benjamin Rush, with some assistance from Mrs. Adams. They resumed writing to each other, but instead of revolution, war, and diplomacy, their former concerns as active statesmen, they discussed philosophy, religion, history, and science.

134

The Spur of fame : dialogues of John Adams and Benjamin Rush, 1805–1813 / edited by John A. Schutz and Douglass Adair. — San Marino, Calif. : Huntington Library, 1966. — viii, 301 p. : ill.

E322 .A5186

In the eighteenth century a common trait of men in public life was the desire for fame—the honor and immortality posterity owes to those who contribute greatly to society, and especially to the founding of a nation. By 1805, when Adams initiated the present correspondence, he and Rush both felt ignored and even abused by a public that gave its highest honors to others who had, they thought, less claim to them. In these letters each candidly reflects on his part in the establishment of the new nation, on the roles of Washington, Jefferson, Hamilton, and others, and on the future of the country.

135

John Adams, 1735–1826 : chronology, documents [and] bibliographical aids / edited by Howard F. Bremer. — Dobbs Ferry, N.Y. : Oceana Publications, 1967. — v, 88 p. — (Oceana presidential chronology series ; 2)

E321 .B8

Bibliography: p. 81–86.

136

John Adams : a biography in his own words / edited by James Bishop Peabody, with an introd. by L. H. Butterfield ; Joan Paterson Kerr, picture editor. — New York : Newsweek ; distributed by Harper & Row, [1973]. — 416 p. : ill. — (The Founding Fathers)

E322 .A35 1973

Bibliography: p. 408.
Brief selections from the diary, autobiography, letters, and public papers arranged in chronological form, with a connecting narrative by the editor.

137

Letters from a distinguished American : twelve essays by John Adams on American foreign policy, 1780 / compiled and edited by James H. Hutson. — Washington : Library of Congress, 1978. — xx, 66 p. : port.

E203 .A57

Includes bibliographical references.
While Adams was in France attempting to negotiate a peace treaty with Britain he wrote this series of essays demonstrating that it was in Britain's long-term interest to settle with its former colonies. These were published in a friendly British newspaper and attributed only to a "distinguished American."

BIOGRAPHIES AND OTHER STUDIES

(Entries are arranged chronologically by date of publication.)

138
Walsh, Correa Moylan.
The political science of John Adams : a study in the theory of mixed government and the bicameral system / by Correa Moylan Walsh. — New York : Putnam, 1915. — xii p., 374 p.

JK171.A3 W3

Reprinted in New York by Books for Libraries Press in 1969.
Adams's political theories are described as a background for the author's defense of bicameralism.

139
Boston Public Library. Adams Collection.
Catalogue of the John Adams library in the Public Library of the City of Boston / edited by Lindsay Swift. — Boston : The Trustees, 1917. — viii, 271 p.

Z881 .B752A

The Adams library was presented to the town of Quincy, Massachusetts, in 1822 and was first housed there and then deposited in the Boston Public Library in 1894.

140
Chinard, Gilbert.
Honest John Adams / by Gilbert Chinard. — Boston : Little, Brown, 1933. — xii p., 3 leaves, [3]–359 p. : front., plates, ports.

E322 .C47

Reprinted in Boston by Little, Brown in 1964.
Long considered the standard one-volume biography of Adams.

141
Cronin, John William.
A bibliography of John Adams and John Quincy Adams / compiled by John W. Cronin and W. Harvey Wise, Jr. — Washington : Riverford Pub. Co., 1935. — 78 p.

Z8015.6 .C91

142
Haraszti, Zoltan.
John Adams & the prophets of progress. — Cambridge : Harvard University Press, 1952. — viii, 362 p. : port., facsims.

E322 .H3

Adams owned one of the largest libraries in the country and made great use of it. He annotated many of the volumes so heavily that the effect is one of a dialogue with the authors. Haraszti uses these notes, which can be the length of short essays, as the basis for an analysis of Adams's thought.

143
Iacuzzi, Alfred.
John Adams, scholar. — New York : S. F. Vanni (Ragusa), [1952]. — 306 p.

E322 .I15

"Bibliographical notes and references": p. 268–296.
Traces the influence of European (mostly French and Italian) thinkers on Adams's theories of law, government, economics, and politics.

144
Butterfield, L.H. (Lyman Henry)
The papers of the Adams family : some account of their history / L. H. Butterfield. — In Massachusetts Historical Society. Proceedings. — Vol. 71 (Oct. 1953–May 1957) ; p. 328–356.

F61 .M38 v. 71

Contains much of interest that is not repeated in the author's introduction to Vol. 1 of the *Diary and Autobiography of John Adams*, especially concerning the accumulation of the family archive, the use made of it, and the attitudes of various family members toward it.

145
Dauer, Manning Julian.
The Adams Federalists. — Baltimore : Johns Hopkins Press, 1953. — xxiii, 381 p. : maps.

E321 .D23

Bibliography: p. 351–373.
Reprinted in Baltimore by Johns Hopkins Press in 1968.
Examines the foreign and domestic policies Adams pursued as president and relates them to the split in the Federalist party between his followers, who tended to be involved in agriculture, and Hamilton's who, along with their leader, were willing to sacrifice the agrarian interest to the commercial.

146
Kurtz, Stephen G.
The presidency of John Adams : the collapse of Federalism, 1795–1800. — Philadelphia : University of Pennsylvania Press, [1957]. — 448 p. : ill.

E321 .K8

Bibliography: p. 417–440.
Adams's presidency was marked by his efforts to avoid a full-fledged war with France and by a growing conflict with Hamilton. The latter controlled a substantial wing of the Federalist party and favored a military build-up, the suppression of domestic dissent, and war with France. Despite the antipathy of most of Adams's own cabinet toward his policies, he did achieve a peace with France. The cost was a further alienation of the Hamiltonians, and ultimately the demise of the Federalist party.

FIGURE 13.   Abigail Adams, From a Portrait by Gilbert Stuart.   (LC–USZ62–2045)

FIGURE 14. View of Home of John and Abigail Adams, Quincy, Massachusetts. (LC–USZ62–96042)

147
Smith, Page.
  John Adams. — Garden City, N.Y. : Doubleday, 1962.
  — 2 v. (xx, 1170 p.) : ill., ports., facsims.
                                          E322 .S64
  Includes bibliographical references.
  Contents: v. 1. 1735–1784 — v. 2. 1784–1826.
  The first full-length scholarly biography of Adams to appear
after the unsealing and publication of the Adams papers, this is
generally considered the standard treatment of his life.

148
Kurtz, Stephen G.
  The French mission of 1799–1800 : concluding chapter in the statecraft of John Adams. — In Political science
quarterly. — Vol. 80 (Dec. 1965) ; p. 543–547.
                                          H1 .P8, v. 80
  Adams considered the peace negotiations with France
one of his greatest achievements, though it split the Federalist party and may have cost him reelection.

149
Allison, John Murray.
  Adams and Jefferson : the story of a friendship. — Norman
: University of Oklahoma Press, [1966]. — 349 p. : ports.
                                          E322 .A6
  Bibliographical footnotes.
  A joint biography, emphasizing more the personal than
the political side of their long relationship.

150
Howe, John R.
  The changing political thought of John Adams / by
John R. Howe, Jr. — Princeton : Princeton University
Press, 1966. — xv, 259 p.
                                          E322 .H6
  "Bibliographical Essay": p. [253]–254 ; Bibliographical
footnotes.
  The need to maintain order and stability in society was the
guiding principle of Adams's political thought, which was
shaped more by experience than ideology. In his early career he
perceived Americans as a uniquely moral people with strong
social cohesion. The turmoil and social conflict of the 1780s
which he saw as signs of moral decline, caused him to alter his
philosophy. Americans were not essentially different from other
nations after all, and so he began to turn from democratic to
aristocratic solutions to the problems of governance.

151
Binder, Frederick M.
  **The color problem in early national America as
viewed by John Adams, Jefferson and Jackson**. — The
Hague ; Paris : Mouton, 1968 [1969]. — 180 p. —
(Studies in American history ; 7)
                                          E184.A1 B55
  Bibliography: p. [163]–169.
  Adams gave no evidence of racism in his behavior or
thought. Although he personally abhorred slavery and
wished for its eventual abolition, he was unwilling to inter-
fere in what he saw as a matter of property rights.

152
Kurtz, Stephen G.
  The political science of John Adams : a guide to his
statecraft. — In William and Mary quarterly. — 3rd ser.
Vol. 25 (Oct. 1968) ; p. 605–613.
                                F221 .W71, 3rd ser. v. 25
  Discusses some of Adams's writings and some of the
books about his philosophy of government.

153
Brown, Ralph A.
  The presidency of John Adams / by Ralph Adams
Brown. — Lawrence : University Press of Kansas, [1975].
  — x, 248 p., [1] leaf of plates : port. — (American Presidency series)
                                          E321 .B84
  Bibliography: p. 233–243.
  Our ideas of the Adams presidency have been shaped, at
least until recently, largely by the writings of his opponents,
much to the detriment of his reputation. In fact, Adams was
successful in avoiding both foreign war and domestic strife,
either of which might have destroyed the infant republic.
He held to his principles and pursued the policies he
thought wise despite harsh criticism from much of his
party, from the press, and from some of his own counselors.

154
Handler, Edward.
  "Nature itself is all arcanum" : the scientific outlook of
John Adams. — In American Philosophical Society. Pro-
ceedings. — Vol. 120 (1976 : no. 3) ; p. 216–227.
                                          Q11 .P8, v. 120
  An often overlooked facet of Adams's personality, his in-
terest in the physical universe, is explored here.

155
Shaw, Peter.
  The character of John Adams / by Peter Shaw. —
Chapel Hill : Published for the Institute of Early American History and Culture, Williamsburg, Va., by the University of North Carolina Press, c1976. — ix, 324 p., [3]
leaves of plates : port.
                                          E322 .S54
  Includes bibliographical references and index.
  Two conflicting elements in Adams's character were his
reverence for proper authority and his strong sense of personal independence; the latter caused him to rebel against
authority from time to time, the former drove him to justify
his rebellion by questioning the legitimacy of the authority.
He could lead a revolution against the king, but only if he
could convince himself and others that the king's actions
contravened the British constitution. He sought recognition
and distinction, but not at the cost of his independence of
thought and action, behavior that earned him a reputation
for contentiousness. This intellectual biography of Adams
examines his reading, his thought, and his motivations.

156

Taylor, Robert J.

John Adams : legalist as revolutionist. — In Massachusetts Historical Society. Proceedings. — Vol. 89 (1977) ; p. 55–71.

F61 .M38, v. 89

Analyzes Adams's revolutionary era writings to show his movement toward the idea of independence.

157

East, Robert Abraham.

John Adams / by Robert A. East. — Boston : Twayne Publishers, 1979. — 126 p. : port. — (Twayne's world leaders series ; TWLS 78)

E322 .E27

Bibliography: p. 119–123.

Concise sketch of Adams's life, career, and character.

158

Hutson, James H.

John Adams and the diplomacy of the American Revolution / James H. Hutson. — Lexington : University Press of Kentucky, c1980. — vii, 199 p.

E249 .H87

Bibliography: p. 191–192.

Influenced by traditional European concepts of diplomacy, Adams and other American emissaries followed conventional diplomatic practice, abandoning it only for compelling reasons, as Adams finally did in the Netherlands when he feared a conspiracy was at work to reduce America to a French dependency.

FAMILY, HOMES, AND HAUNTS

159

Adams, Abigail Smith.

Letters of Mrs. Adams, the wife of John Adams / with an introductory memoir by her grandson, Charles Francis Adams. — 4th ed., rev. and enl. — Boston : Wilkins, Carter, 1848. — lxi p., 1 leaf, 472 p. : front. (port.), facsim.

E322.1 .A32

160

New letters of Abigail Adams, 1788–1801 / edited and with an introd. by Stewart Mitchell. — Boston : Houghton Mifflin Co., 1947. — xiii, 281 p. : ill., ports., geneal. tables.

E322.1 .A37

Includes bibliographies.

Reprinted in Westport, Conn., by Greenwood Press in 1973.

Letters written to the author's sister, Mary Cranch, reprinted from the *Proceedings of the American Antiquarian Society*, Vol. 55, p. [95]–332 ; [299]–444.

161

The Book of Abigail and John : selected letters of the Adams family, 1762–1784 / edited and with an introd. by L. H. Butterfield, Marc Friedlaender, and Mary-Jo Kline. — Cambridge, Mass. : Harvard University Press, 1975. — ix, 411 p., [1] leaf of plates : ill.

E322.1 .A293

A different sampling from that compiled by Charles Francis Adams (see above), including much that he edited out for reasons of propriety and decorum. Some letters to other persons and some diary and autobiographical passages which illuminate their relationship are included.

162

Shepherd, Jack.

The Adams chronicles : four generations of greatness / Jack Shepherd ; introd. by Daniel J. Boorstin. — Boston : Little, Brown, c1975. — xxxi, 448 p. : ill.

E322.1.A28 S53

Bibliography: p. 433–436.

Narrative of the lives and careers of the more prominent family members and their spouses.

163

Akers, Charles W.

Abigail Adams, an American woman / Charles W. Akers. — Boston : Little, Brown, c1980. — x, 207 p., [1] leaf of plates : ill. — (The Library of American biography)

E322.1.A38 A35

Bibliography: p. [193]–200.

164

Withey, Lynne.

Dearest friend : a life of Abigail Adams / Lynne Withey. — New York : Free Press ; London : Collier Macmillan, c1981. — xiv, 369 p., [8] p. of plates : ill.

E322.1.A38 W56

Bibliography: p. [347]–356.

165

Harris, Wilhelmina S.

Adams National Historic Site : a family's legacy to America / Wilhelmina S. Harris. — Washington : U.S. Dept. of the Interior. National Park Service, 1983. — xi, 64 p. : ill. (some col.).

F74.Q7 H24 1983

166

Nagel, Paul C.

Descent from glory : four generations of the John Adams family / Paul C. Nagel. — New York : Oxford University Press, 1983. — xiv, 400 p., [12] p. of plates : ill.

CS71 .A2 1983

Includes bibliographical references and index.

Emphasizes the often difficult relationships among members of the family and their internal conflicts rather than their public careers. Individual weaknesses, unfortunate marriages, and unrealistic expectations often brought pain to all.

167

Levin, Phyllis Lee.

Abigail Adams : a biography / Phyllis Lee Levin. — New York : St. Martin's Press, 1987. — xv, 575 p., [16] p. of plates : ill., ports.

E322.1.A38 L48 1987

Bibliography: p. [551]–556.

168

Nagel, Paul C.

The Adams women : Abigail and Louisa Adams, their sisters and daughters / Paul C. Nagel. — New York : Oxford University Press, 1987. — viii, 310 p., [12] p. of plates : ill.

E322.1.A38 N34 1987

Bibliography: p. 297–302.

Abigail and Louisa (the wife of John Quincy Adams) typify the change in the roles of American women as the country moved from its decentralized agrarian past into an urban, industrial era. The former was her husband's partner and confidante in virtually all his activities from farming to politics; the latter, though competent and able, was restricted by her husband and by new societal expectations about middle-class women's proper role to a narrow domestic life.

FIGURE 15.   Drawing of Thomas Jefferson by Benjamin Henry Latrobe, ca. 1802.   (LC–USZ61–1105)

Chapter III

Thomas Jefferson

Compiled by Marilyn K. Parr

WRITINGS OF THOMAS JEFFERSON

(Entries are arranged chronologically by date of publication.)

Collected Writings

169

Memoir, correspondence, and miscellanies : from the papers of Thomas Jefferson / ed. by Thomas Jefferson Randolph. — Charlottesville [Va.] : F. Carr and co., 1829. — 4 v. : front. port., facsims. (part fold.).

E302 .J458

Published just three years after Jefferson's death, this first edition of his papers was prepared by his grandson, Thomas Jefferson Randolph. As executor of the estate, Randolph was bequeathed a comprehensive collection of Jefferson's papers; and in this edition, he has presented both public and private letters, the Memoirs, the Anas and a facsimile of the Declaration of Independence written in his grandfather's hand. In the same year Randolph supervised the Library of Congress acquisition of Jefferson's collection of works on Virginia history. Twenty years later the United States government purchased Randolph's Jefferson collection for deposit in the State Department, where it remained until the 1904 transfer to the Library of Congress. The letters in these volumes are only a portion of the Jefferson material available to modern historians; however, they form the basis for the numerous editions that have been published since 1829.

170

The Writings of Thomas Jefferson : being his autobiography, correspondence, reports, messages, addresses, and other writings, official and private / ed. by Henry Augustine Washington. — Washington : Taylor and Maury, 1853–54. — 9 v. : ill., front. port.

E302 .J464

Contents: v. 1. Autobiography, with appendix Correspondence — v. 2.–6. Correspondence — v. 7. Correspondence cont. Reports and opinions while secretary of state — v. 8. Inaugural addresses and messages. Replies to public addresses. Indian addresses. Miscellaneous: 1. Notes on Virginia; 2. Biographical sketches of distinguished men; 3. the batture at New Orleans — v. 9. Miscellaneous: Parliamentary manual; 5. The Anas; 6. Miscellaneous papers.

In 1850 the congressional Joint Committee on the Library asked Henry Augustine Washington, a professor at the College of William and Mary, to prepare a new edition of the Jefferson papers for publication. The Committee further advised that "It is not expected or desired that any editorial matter should be incorporated" and that Professor Washington should select letters of a "public" nature. In order to accommodate the chosen editor, the State Department had the entire collection moved to the college where 40,000 Jefferson letters were read and rearranged in four years. Although this edition contains more letters than the first edition, the published volumes reflect the committee's instructions about content. Thus there are few explanatory comments by Professor Washington. The editor has been criticized for his careless handling of the letters and his dismantling of Jefferson's arrangement of his papers.

171

The Writings of Thomas Jefferson / collected and edited by Paul Leicester Ford. — New York : G. P. Putnam's sons, 1892–99. — 10 v.

E302 .J466

Contents: v. 1. 1760–1775 — v. 2. 1776–1781 — v. 3. 1781–1784 — v. 4. 1784–1787 — v. 5. 1788–1792 — v. 6. 1792–1794 — v. 7. 1795–1801 — v. 8. 1801–1806 — v. 9. 1807–1815 — v. 10. 1816–1826.

"Federal edition" reprinted in twelve volumes in 1904–1905.

By 1888 serious questions were raised by a great-granddaughter, Sarah N. Randolph, and others about the quality of Henry Washington's work. She proposed a new edition in order to incorporate the personal letters in her family's possession as well as the public papers of Jefferson at the State Department. Miss Randolph died before Congress authorized another edition; however, Paul Leicester Ford continued Miss Randolph's ideas in the third published collection of the Jefferson papers. Ford used the existing letters in addition to letters retained in numerous institutions and private collections to prepare a more comprehensive edition and to correct Professor Washington's errors. These volumes remain useful because of the careful editing techniques.

172

The Writings of Thomas Jefferson : containing his autobiography, notes on Virginia, parliamentary manual, official and private, now collected and published in their entirety for the first time, including all of the original manuscripts, deposited in the Department of State, and published in 1853 by order of the Joint Committee of Congress; with numerous illustrations and a comprehensive analytic index / Andrew A. Lipscomb, editor-in-chief ; Albert Ellery Bergh, managing editor. — Memorial ed. — Washington : issued under the auspices of the Thomas Jefferson Memorial Association of the United States, 1903–04. — 20 v. : fronts., plates, ports., fold. map, facsims. (part fold.).

E302 .J472

"A contribution to a bibliography of Thomas Jefferson, compiled by Richard Holland Johnston": v. 20 (iv, 73 p.).

Continuing the work of Paul L. Ford, the Lipscomb and Bergh edition expands on the previous work by adding new correspondence and miscellaneous writings of the third president. The editors published the most inclusive compilation of Jefferson's papers at the time, but they relied on Henry Washington's text and thus prolonged his errors and omissions. This was considered the standard work on Jefferson until after 1950.

173

Papers / Julian P. Boyd, editor ; Lyman H. Butterfield [and others] associate editors. — Princeton : Princeton University Press, 1950– <1992 >. — v. <1–26 > : ill., ports., maps, facsims.

E302 .J442 1950a

The purpose of this fifth compilation of Jefferson's papers states a deceptively simple task: "this work is to present the writings and recorded actions of Thomas Jefferson as accurately and as completely as possible." In 1943 when the project started at Princeton University the editors projected a minimum of fifty volumes in two series. The first, a chronological series of every available letter written by or to Jefferson, was created to include messages, speeches, travel journals, minutes of proceedings, etc. Series two was to consist of the other writings of Jefferson such as *Notes on the State of Virginia*, and *Manual of Parliamentary Practice*, arranged in a classified scheme. Jefferson's papers have been presented in many formats and arrangements; however, Boyd and Butterfield conjectured that less than one-third of the total had been published. Twenty-six volumes of the chronological series have been completed and three volumes of the second series are available. These latter volumes are entered separately in this bibliography. Paul Sifton notes in his description of the Jefferson papers deposited at the Library of Congress: "The Boyd volumes will attempt, in printed form, to restore the Jefferson papers to the archival care and historiographical thoroughness which they possessed when Jefferson bequeathed them to his favorite grandson."

Selected Writings

174

The Jeffersonian cyclopedia : a comprehensive collection of the views of Thomas Jefferson classified and arranged in alphabetical order under nine thousand titles relating to government, politics, law, education, political economy, finance, science, art, literature, religious freedom, morals, etc. / ed. by John P. Foley. — New York ; London : Funk & Wagnalls co., 1900. — 4 p. leaves, [xiii]–xxii, [2], 1009 p. : front., plates, ports.

JK113 .J4 1900

Quoting Jefferson's writings on various topics, this volume utilized three printed sources; *The Writings of Thomas Jefferson* edited by Henry A. Washington, *The Writings of Thomas Jefferson* edited by Paul Leicester Ford, and Sarah N. Randolph's *Domestic Life of Jefferson*. The subject entries are arranged in alphabetical order followed by an appendix of miscellaneous writings and a separate cross-referenced topical index. The dated language hinders the value of the work but a contemporary edition does not exist.

175

The Jefferson papers [1770–1826]. In Massachusetts Historical Society. Collections. — Boston, 1900 (ser. 7, v. 1). — xxxvii, 389 p.

F61 .M41, ser. 7, v. 1

The Jefferson papers deposited by Thomas Jefferson Randolph with the State Department in 1848 were to be thoroughly examined in order to separate the public from the private papers. The private material was eventually returned to the Randolph family in 1870 and 1871. In 1898 Thomas Jefferson Coolidge, a great-grandson of Jefferson, purchased seven thousand items from his Randolph cousins which he then presented to the Massachusetts Historical Society. The miscellaneous selections of the volume are incorporated into the Princeton edition of Jefferson's papers.

176

Thomas Jefferson correspondence / printed from the originals in the collections of William K. Bixby ; with notes by Worthington Chauncey Ford. — Boston : s.n., 1916. — xiv p., 1 leaf, 322 p. : facsims. (part fold., incl. front.)

E302 .J57

After completing his edition of Jefferson's papers, Henry A. Washington was thought to have returned the entire collection to the State Department. However, in 1912, the heir of Washington's coeditor, George Tucker, sold 2,500 Jefferson items to William K. Bixby. It is probable that these items came from the Jefferson papers relinquished to Washington in 1850. Unfortunately Bixby divided his purchase among forty-seven institutions and repositories and this volume reproduces only a selection of the original items.

177

Official letters of the governors of the state of Virginia.
— Richmond : D. Bottom, superintendent of public
printing, 1926–1929. — 3 v. : fold. facsim.

F221 .V6 v. 2

Jefferson letters, June 1, 1779–June 3, 1781.

Although the letters for this period are part of the Princeton edition (no. 173), the utility of a single compilation of
Governor Jefferson's correspondence should not be under-
valued. The printed or manuscript source of each item is
included as well as numerous footnotes that clarify questions about Virginia legislative history.

178

The Complete Jefferson : containing his major writings,
published and unpublished, except his letters / assem-
bled and arranged by Saul K. Padover, with illustrations
and analytic index. — New York : Distributed by Duell,
Sloan & Pearce, [1943]. — xxix p., 1 leaf, 1322 p. : ill.,
front. (port.), facsims.

E302 .J4564

"Selected Bibliography": p. 1301–1302.

This earliest and most complete, to date, compilation of
Jefferson's public papers will eventually be superceded by the
Princeton edition (no. 173). Arranged by broad subject areas,
the writings are printed in chronological order with personal
letters inserted where deemed necessary by the editor.

179

Thomas Jefferson, revolutionary philosopher : a selection
of writings / edited by John S. Pancake with N. Sharon
Summers. — A Bicentennial ed. — Woodbury, N.Y. : Bar-
ron's Educational Series, c1976. — 346 p. : ill.

E302 .J59

The editors have prepared a balanced introduction to Jefferson's views spanning the following subjects: the presidency, diplomacy, education, religion, American Indians,
and African Americans.

180

Jefferson, magnificent populist / Martin A. Larson. —
Washington : R.B. Luce, c1981. — xxiv, 390 p.

E302 .J442 1981

Bibliography: p. xiv.

Based on secondary sources, this compilation of selective
quotations reflects the author's belief that Jefferson spoke
for the common man rather than the social and political
aristocracy of post-revolutionary America. Brief commen-
taries preface the self-contained chapters.

181

Writings / Thomas Jefferson. — New York : Literary Clas-
sics of the U.S. : Distributed to the trade in the U.S. and
Canada by the Viking Press, c1984. — 1600 p. : map. —
(The Library of America ; 17)

E302 .J442 1984

Bibliographic notes: p. 1532–1579.

Contents: Autobiography — A summary view of the
rights of British America — Notes on the State of Virginia
— Public papers — Addresses, messages, and replies —
Miscellany — Letters.

"Merrill D. Peterson wrote the notes and selected the
texts for this volume."

Writings are published in full from editions either supervised by or contemporary to Jefferson.

182

A Summary view of the rights of British America : set forth
in some resolutions intended for the inspection of the present delegates of the people of Virginia. Now in convention
/ By a native and member of the House of Burgesses. —
Williamsburg : Printed by Clementina Rind, [1774]. — 23
p. — (Colonial Pamphlets ; v. 12, no. 2)

E211 .J44 Rare Bk. Coll.

Written as draft instructions for the Virginia delegates to
the First Continental Congress, the Summary View was fa-
vorably received; however, the language was considered too
radical to be used officially. Jefferson's supporters had the
document printed without his knowledge, thus adding Jefferson's voice to the growing pamphlet literature calling for
colonial independence.

183

Notes on the state of Virginia / written by Thomas Jefferson ; illustrated with a map, including the states of Virginia, Maryland, Delaware and Pennsylvania. — 2nd
English edition. — London : J. Stockdale, 1787. — 2
leaves, 382 p. : tables, front. (fold. map), fold. tab.

F230 .J41 Rare Bk. Coll.

Reprinted in Williamsburg, Va., for the Institute of Early
American Culture by the University of North Carolina Press
in 1955 (F230 .J5102 1955).

Published in response to queries from François de Barbe-
Marbois, secretary to the French legation for information,
the notes cover all aspects of life in Virginia. Jefferson describes not only geography and agriculture, but also the
laws, religion, culture, and history of his native state. Privately printed in 1784–85 in Paris, the work has been
reprinted as a monograph and it appears frequently in collected works of Jefferson. A modern edition is to be published in the second series of the Princeton edition.

184

**An Essay towards facilitating instruction in the Anglo-
Saxon and modern dialects of the English language** :
For the use of the University of Virginia. — New York : J.
F. Trow, printer, 1851. — 43 p.

PE123 .J3

Consisting of a letter to Henry Croft, October 30, 1798,
and short essays about the Anglo-Saxon dialect and grammar, this collection provides evidence for Jefferson's belief
in studying Anglo-Saxon in order to better understand English. A course in the language was part of the early curricu-
lum at the University of Virginia.

185

The Complete anas of Thomas Jefferson / ed. by Franklin B. Sawvel. — New York : Round Table Press, 1903. — 283 p. : front. plates, 2 port., 2 facsim.

E310 .J45

Composed of "loose scraps of paper, taken out of my pocket in the moment, and laid by to be copied fair at leisure, which, however, they hardly ever were," the Anas was a compilation of these jottings from 1793 to 1807. Jefferson further explains that he bound the "scraps" at one time, then rearranged them in 1818 removing papers where he deemed necessary. This particular edition, as well as earlier printings, lacks the textual analysis and extensive annotations of modern historical editing projects.

Individual Works

186

Jefferson et les idéologues d'après sa correspondance inédite avec Destutt de Tracy, Cabanis, J.B. Say et Auguste Comte / par Gilbert Chinard. — Baltimore : The Johns Hopkins Press ; Paris : Les Presses Universitaires de France, 1925. — 2 p. leaves, 295, [1] p. — (The Johns Hopkins studies in romance literature and language ; extra vol. 1)

E332 .C53

"Ouvrages Consultés": p. [288]–291.

Although the text is in French, the Jefferson letters in this compilation, which spans the years 1802 to 1826, are printed in the original English. The bibliography is particularly useful in listing unfamiliar sources in both languages.

187

The Commonplace book of Thomas Jefferson : a repertory of his ideas on government / with an introduction and notes by Gilbert Chinard. — Baltimore and Paris : The John [!] Hopkins press and Les Presses Universitaires de France, 1926. — 3 p. leaves, 403 [1] p. — (The John (!) Hopkins studies in romance literature and languages ; extra vol. II)

E302 .J454

Including over nine hundred entries transcribed by Jefferson from legal and political writings of the period, this work is separate and distinct from the Literary Commonplace Book (no. 200). Beginning as early as 1764 and continuing until after 1801, Jefferson recorded selections of interest from Montesquieu, Voltaire, Helvetius, William Eden, Lord Kames, and other noted jurists.

188

Trois amitiés françaises de Jefferson : d'après sa correspondance inédite avec Madame de Bréhan, Madame de Tessé et Madame de Corny / [par] Gilbert Chinard. — Paris : Société d'édition "Les Belles lettres," 1927. — vi, 242 p., 1 leaf.

E332 .C54

"Bibliographie": p. [241]–242.

Repeating the pattern in his earlier work, a French text with Jefferson's letters printed in the original English, Chinard focuses on the correspondence of three socially prominent French women who knew Jefferson in Paris. The bibliography sets forth some infrequently consulted sources.

189

The Letters of Lafayette and Jefferson / with an introduction and notes by Gilbert Chinard. — Baltimore : The Johns Hopkins Press ; Paris : "Les Belles lettres," 1929. — xiv p., 3 leaves, (5)–443 p. incl. front. (port.). : map, facsims. — (The Johns Hopkins studies in international thought)

E207.L2 L18

This continuation of the editor's study of Jefferson and France brings together previously unpublished letters for the years 1781 to 1826. Careful editing and full annotations complete the text in which Lafayette's letters are printed in the original French.

190

The Correspondence of Jefferson and Du Pont de Nemours / with an introduction on Jefferson and the physiocrats, by Gilbert Chinard. — Baltimore : The Johns Hopkins Press ; Paris : "Les Belles lettres," 1931. — 3 p. leaves, [ix]–cxxii, 293 p. : ill., front., port. — (The Johns Hopkins studies in international thought)

E302 .J427

Reprinted in New York by Burt Franklin in 1971.

Following an extensive introduction discussing eighteenth-century French intellectualism and the effect, if any, on Jefferson, the editor has organized the letters, 1787–1817, in chronological order with few explanatory notes. The Du Pont letters are printed in French and Jefferson's in English. Dumas Malone's edition of the same correspondence (*Correspondence Between Thomas Jefferson and Pierre Samuel Du Pont De Nemours*, Boston, Houghton Mifflin, 1930) translates the Du Pont letters and provides footnotes for the general reader.

191

Correspondence of Thomas Jefferson and Francis Walker Gilmer, 1814–1826 / edited, with an introduction, by Richard Beale Davis. — Columbia : University of South Carolina Press, 1946. — 163 p. : ill., front., port., facsims.

E332 .J447

"Textual and Bibliographical Note": p. 25 ; Bibliography: p. 157–158.

Records the relationship between the correspondents and Gilmer's role in securing faculty for the University of Virginia in 1824. A biographical sketch places the young lawyer within Jefferson's circle and further defines Gilmer's connection with the intellectuals of the early republic. The editor has included the source of each letter and explanatory notes where necessary.

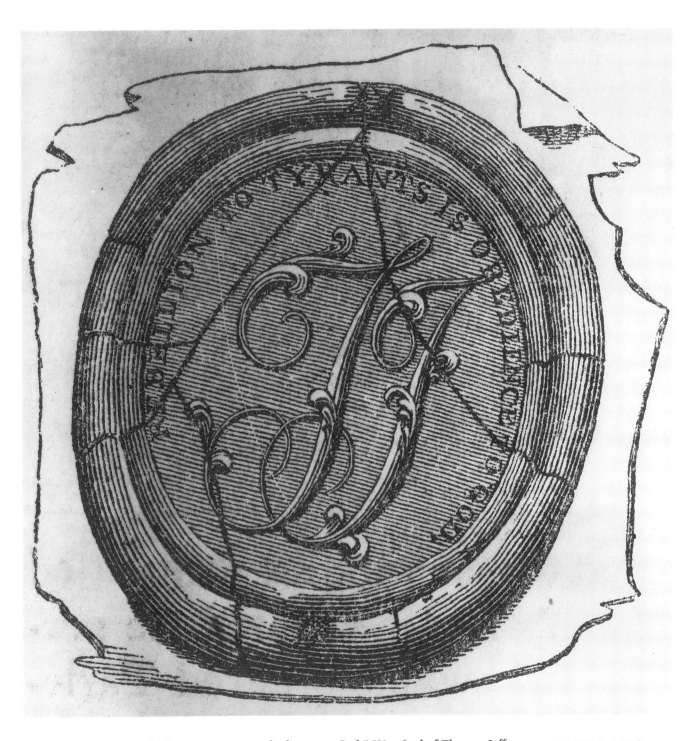

FIGURE 16. "Rebellion to tyrants is obedience to God," Wax Seal of Thomas Jefferson. (LC–USZ62–45715)

FIGURE 17. Monticello. (LC–US262–32441)

192
Dumbauld, Edward.

Thomas Jefferson, American tourist : being an account of his journeys in the United States of America, England, France, Italy, the Low countries, and Germany / by Edward Dumbauld. — Norman : University of Oklahoma Press, 1946. — xv, 266 p., 1 leaf : plates, ports., facsims.

E332 .D8

Bibliography: p. 241–260.

In order to investigate thoroughly the travels of the third president and the locales in which he resided, the author personally followed Jefferson's itinerary throughout the United States and Europe recording his own impressions of these areas. The appendix includes a chronological list of Jefferson's official and informal journeys from 1775 to 1809 when he retired to Monticello.

193

Jefferson's ideas on a university library : letters from the founder of the University of Virginia to a Boston bookseller / edited by Elizabeth Cometti. — Charlottesville : Tracy W. McGregor Library, University of Virginia, 1950. — 49 p.

Z733.V72 J4 Rare Bk. Coll.

"Bibliographical Note": p. 14–15.

Published 125 years after the opening of the University of Virginia, this work records both the process by which the library collections were selected and the establishment of a bookstore for the University community. The correspondence (1824–1826) between Jefferson and his Boston book dealer, William Hilliard of Cummings, Hilliard and Co., sheds light on Jefferson's ideas about book publishing in general and libraries in particular.

194

The Adams-Jefferson letters : the complete correspondence between Thomas Jefferson and Abigail and John Adams / edited by Lester J. Cappon. — Chapel Hill : Published for the Institute of Early American History and Culture at Williamsburg, Va., by the University of North Carolina Press, [1959]. — 2 v. (638 p.). : ill., ports.

E322 .A516

Reprinted in Chapel Hill by the University of North Carolina Press in 1988.

Recording a relationship of over fifty years the letters between Jefferson and Adams reflect the development of their ideals, the turmoils and triumphs of diplomatic service and high political office, and the formation of the United States. These letters will be reproduced as part of the Princeton edition; however, there is an integrity within the relationship that warrants a separate edition of this correspondence.

195

The Jefferson-Dunglison letters / edited by John M. Dorsey. — Charlottesville : University of Virginia Press, [1960]. — 120 p. : port.

E332.88 .D75

Studies the relationship between Dr. Robley Dunglison, professor of anatomy and chairman of the faculty of the University of Virginia, and the founder of the institution. Dunglison, a British citizen, who was selected by Francis Gilmer to join the University became Jefferson's personal physician during the last months of his life.

196

Thomas Jefferson and his unknown brother / edited and introduced by Bernard Mayo ; with additions by James A. Bear, Jr. — Charlottesville : University Press of Virginia, 1981. — viii, 59 p. : map.

E332.88 .J4 1981

First published in 1942 (E332 .J475).

The thirty-two letters reproduced here are the only extant items from the fifty or more letters written between 1789 and 1815. Most are from the Carr-Cary papers of the McGregor Library, University of Virginia; three are from the Massachusetts Historical Society, and one is from the Library of Congress.

The scant biographical information known about Randolph Jefferson (1755–1815) is provided in the introduction, with footnotes completing the details of Jefferson family affairs.

197

Jefferson's extracts from the Gospels : "The philosophy of Jesus" and "The life and morals of Jesus" / Dickinson W. Adams, editor ; Ruth W. Lester, assistant editor ; introduction by Eugene R. Sheridan. — Princeton, N.J. : Princeton University Press, c1983. — xii, 438 p. : facsims. — (The Papers of Thomas Jefferson ; 2nd ser.)

BS2549.J5 J43 1983

"The Philosophy" has been carefully reconstructed from Jefferson's notes on the subject and "The Life and Morals" has been reproduced from the original held at the Smithsonian Institution. Thorough annotations complement the text and the appendix includes the Jefferson correspondence between 1800 and 1824 relevant to his personal religious views.

198

The Garden and farm books of Thomas Jefferson / edited by Robert C. Baron. — Golden, Colo. : Fulcrum, c1987. — 528 p. : ill. (some col.), facsims.

SB451.34.V8 J44 1987

Bibliography: p. [513]–519.

Reproduces the original Jefferson notebooks that recorded his thoughts about agriculture, both practical and theoretical, and his observations of seasonal change at Monticello. The notes, housed at the Massachusetts Historical Society, were previously edited by Edwin M. Betts, as *Thomas Jefferson's Garden Book, 1766–1824* (1944) and *Thomas Jefferson's Farm Book* (1953), whose work complements this edition.

199

Jefferson's parliamentary writings : Parliamentary pocket-book and A Manual of parliamentary practice / edited with an introduction by Wilbur Samuel Howell. — Princeton, N.J. : Princeton University Press, c1988. — xxix, 454 p. : [4] p. plates, facsims. — (The Papers of Thomas Jefferson ; 2nd ser.)

KF4982 .J44 1988

Includes bibliographical references and index.

Printed for the first time, the pocket-book contains Jefferson's transcriptions taken from his reading on two subjects: incidental parliamentary procedure and constitutional matters in the British House of Commons. The compilation was begun during the late 1760s and continued while Jefferson was vice president and presiding officer of the Senate. The manual is also a result of his years of legislative experience with the Senate. The editor's notes regarding the location of the manuscripts and Jefferson's numerous marginal notations are representative of the detailed techniques used by the Princeton editors of Jefferson's papers.

200

Jefferson's literary commonplace book / Douglas L. Wilson, editor. — Princeton, N.J. : Princeton University Press, c1989. — xx, 242 p. : ill. — (The Papers of Thomas Jefferson. Second series)

E332.9.C6 J44 1989

Includes bibliographical references and index.

Between 1758 and 1773 Jefferson recorded passages from his reading of Virgil, Homer, and Cicero as well as Shakespeare, Milton, Pope, Dryden, and others into what has become known as his literary bible or literary commonplace book. The exacting standards of modern historical editing are evident in this edition which includes an exhaustive study of Jefferson's handwriting in the original text and a descriptive analysis of the manuscript. A register of authors identifies the editions used by Jefferson; English translations of these texts are placed within the extensive annotations.

Library Catalogs

201

Catalogue of the library of Thomas Jefferson / compiled with annotations by E. Millicent Sowerby. — The Thomas Jefferson Memorial Foundation edition. Reprint with new foreword. — Charlottesville : University Press of Virginia, 1983. — 5 v.

Z881 .U5 1983

Includes bibliographical references and indexes.
Originally published 1952–1959.

Planned in 1942 as part of the bicentennial celebration of the third president's birth, the project was commissioned to recreate the original order of Jefferson's library. The entries are arranged into Jefferson's divisions of knowledge; however, the exact order within the divisions or chapters eluded the editor. Extensive annotations include a physical description of each book, relative quotations from Jefferson's correspondence, and pertinent information about the author, editor, or translator of the works.

202

Gilreath, James.
Thomas Jefferson's library : a catalog with the entries in his own order / edited by James Gilreath and Douglas L. Wilson. — Washington : Library of Congress, 1988. — vii, 149 p. : ill.

Z997.J48 G55 1988

In 1823 Nicholas Trist, at Jefferson's request, rewrote the catalog to the book collection that had been purchased to reestablish the Library of Congress. This restored arrangement reflected the intellectual progression of the works as well as their physical placement on the shelves at Monticello. Gilreath and Wilson have meticulously edited the Trist manuscript and provided an explanation of the text and how it differs from the catalog printed for Congress in 1815.

WORKS ABOUT THOMAS JEFFERSON

(Entries are arranged chronologically by date of publication.)

Bibliographies and Reference Guides

203

Huddleston, Eugene L.
Thomas Jefferson, a reference guide / Eugene L. Huddleston. — Boston, Mass. : G.K. Hall, c1982. — xxiii, 374 p. — (Reference guide to literature)

Z8452.E332 .H8

This extensive annotated bibliography which continues the survey of sources in Merrill Peterson's *The Jefferson Image in the American Mind* claims to list all scholarship about Jefferson written after 1940. Included are monographs, articles, dissertations, and theses. The index is cross-referenced by author and title.

204

Cable, Carole.
Thomas Jefferson, architect : a bibliography of scholarship from 1968–1981 / Carole Cable. — Monticello, Ill. : Vance Bibliographies, [1983]. — 10 p. — (Architecture series—bibliography ; A–995)

Z8452 .C32 1983

A supplement to William Bainter O'Neal's "An Intelligent Interest in Architecture: A Bibliography of Publications about Thomas Jefferson as an Architect," — In American Association of Architectural Bibliographers. Papers. — Vol. 6 (1969), p. 1–150.

FIGURE 18.   Thomas Jefferson, Secretary of State, with President Washington and Secretary of the Treasury Alexander Hamilton, mural by Constantino Brumidi, Senate Reception Room, U.S. Capitol.
(LC–USA7–35116)

205

Shuffelton, Frank.

Thomas Jefferson : a comprehensive, annotated bibliography of writings about him (1826–1980) / Frank Shuffelton. — New York : Garland Pub., 1983. — xix, 486 p. — (Garland reference library of social science ; vol. 184)

Z8452 .S55 1983

Updates previous scholarship on this subject. The author presents critical annotations arranged in chronological order, covering both popular and academic monographs, journal articles, and theses. Subject and author indexes complete the work.

206

Thomas Jefferson : a reference biography / Merrill D. Peterson, editor. — New York : Scribner, c1986. — xiii, 513 p., [1] leaf of plates : ill., col. port.

E332 .T43 1986

Bibliographic essay: p. 453–478.

Brings together twenty-five independent essays that thoroughly explore the many interests and facets of Jefferson. Footnotes have been omitted; however, an extensive bibliographic essay rounds out the work.

General Biographies

207

Tucker, George.

The life of Thomas Jefferson, third president of the United States : with parts of his correspondence never before published and notices of his opinions on questions of civil government, national policy, and constitutional law / by George Tucker. — Philadelphia : Carey, Lea & Blanchard, 1837. — 2 v. : front.

E332 .T89

Written in partial response to three critical works, this first comprehensive examination of Jefferson aimed to present an "accurate and impartial" study of his life. The author, a professor at the University of Virginia, had the advantage of a twenty-seven-year acquaintance with his subject, plus interviews with others who knew the third president firsthand. Sources include the papers held by Thomas Jefferson Randolph and Nicholas P. Trist.

208

Randall, Henry Stephens.

The life of Thomas Jefferson / by Henry S. Randall. — New York : Derby & Jackson, 1858. — 3 v. : fronts. (v. 1–2) ports., facsims. (part fold.).

E332 .R18

Reprinted in Freeport, N.Y., by Books for Libraries Press in 1970 and in New York by Da Capo Press in 1972.

Viewed by some as the most important nineteenth-century work on Jefferson, this is a larger study of the subject than is found in earlier biographies. Sources not available to George Tucker, such as Jefferson's account books, were used to provide new information, and the numerous annotations add much to the text.

209

Adams, Henry.

History of the United States of America. — New York : C. Scribner's sons, 1891–1898. — 9 v.

E302.1 .A23

Recently issued with the title *History of the United States of America during the Administration of Thomas Jefferson* in New York by Literary Classics of the United States, distributed by Viking Press in 1986.

Written by the great-grandson of the second president and the grandson of the sixth, this work is an extensive study of American history between 1801 and 1809.

Partial contents: v. 1–2. The first administration of Thomas Jefferson — v. 3–4. The second administration of Thomas Jefferson.

210

Kimball, Marie Goebel.

Jefferson : the road to glory, 1743 to 1776 / by Marie Kimball. — New York : Coward-McCann, [1943]. — ix, 358 p. : front., plates, ports., map, facsims. (1 double).

E332 .K5

Bibliographical references included in "Notes" (p. 307–335).

Reprinted in Westport, Conn., by Greenwood Press in 1977.

Chronicling the life of the third president up to 1789, Kimball has written three volumes that contributed to Jeffersonian scholarship of the time. Previously unpublished letters supplement the text which studies Jefferson's youth, marriage, and early governmental experience.

211

Kimball, Marie Goebel.

Jefferson, war and peace, 1776 to 1784. — New York : Coward-McCann, [1947]. — ix, 398 p. : plate, ports.

E332 .K52

Bibliographical references included in "Notes" (p. 363–390).

Describes his participation in the Continental Congress and the writing of the Declaration of Independence.

212

Malone, Dumas.

Jefferson and his time. — [1st ed.]. — Boston : Little, Brown, 1948–1981. — 6 v. : ill., ports., maps.

E332 .M25

Includes bibliographies.

Contents: v. 1. Jefferson the Virginian — v. 2. Jefferson and the rights of man — v. 3. Jefferson and the ordeal of liberty — v. 4. Jefferson the president, first term, 1801–1805 — v. 5. Jefferson the president, second term, 1805–1809 — v. 6. The Sage of Monticello.

An exhaustive biography of the subject and his milieu.

213

Kimball, Marie Goebel.

Jefferson : the scene of Europe, 1784 to 1789. — New York : Coward-McCann, [1950]. — ix, 357 p. : ill., ports., map (on lining papers).

E332 .K513 1950

Bibliographical references included in "Notes" (p. 311–342).

214

Peterson, Merrill D.

Thomas Jefferson and the new nation : a biography / [by] Merrill D. Peterson. — New York : Oxford University Press, 1970. — ix, 1072 p. : ill., ports.

E332 .P45

Bibliography: p. [1011]–1047.

Provides an all-encompassing study of Jefferson in a single volume.

215

Cunningham, Noble E.

In pursuit of reason : the life of Thomas Jefferson / Noble E. Cunningham, Jr. — Baton Rouge : Louisiana State University Press, c1987. — xvi, 414 p., [16] p. of plates : ill., ports. — (Southern biography series)

E332 .C95 1987

"Notes and Bibliography": p. [351]–405.

In this one-volume biography, the author portrays Jefferson as a man of the Enlightenment who believed that the use of reason would create a more perfect society. This conviction influenced the third president's political thinking as well as his interests outside government.

Jefferson Portrayed

216

Kimball, Fiske.

The life portraits of Jefferson and their replicas / [by] Sidney Fiske Kimball. — In American Philosophical Society. Proceedings. — Vol. 88 (1944) ; p. 497–534 : ports.

Q11 .P5 v. 88

Includes bibliographic footnotes.

Prepared at the time of the 1943 Thomas Jefferson Bicentennial Exhibition at the National Gallery of Art. The author discusses chronologically the portraits and busts taken during the subject's lifetime. Artists such as Houdin, Gilbert Stuart, John Trumbull, Thomas Sully, and Charles Willson Peale are included, as well as lesser known painters. Many of these items were shown at the 1976 exhibition titled "The Eye of Thomas Jefferson."

217

Cunningham, Noble E.

The image of Thomas Jefferson in the public eye : portraits for the people, 1800–1809 / Noble E. Cunningham, Jr. — Charlottesville : University Press of Virginia, 1981. — xvii, 185 p. : ports.

N7628.J4 C86

Catalogs and describes the significance of a vast array of items including prints, earthenware, medals, and silhouettes displaying Jefferson's image.

A Personal Look

218

Bullock, Helen Claire Duprey.

My head and my heart : a little history of Thomas Jefferson and Maria Cosway / by Helen Duprey Bullock ; with preface by Carleton Sprague Smith. — New York : G.P. Putnam's sons, [1945]. — xvii p., 1 leaf, 235 p. : front., plates, ports.

E332 .B95

Bibliography: p. 210–219.

Although he was always reticent about his personal and family life, Jefferson's friendship with the accomplished Maria Cosway gives a glimpse of the less cerebral side of his nature.

219

Binger, Carl Alfred Lanning.

Thomas Jefferson, a well-tempered mind / by Carl Binger. — [1st ed.]. — New York : Norton, [1970]. — 209 p. : col. port.

E332.2 .B55 1970

Bibliography: p. [197]–198.

This psychohistorical study of Jefferson's life before 1800 deduces that the feminine and masculine characteristics of his personality were well balanced. Such "inner harmony" writes Binger, accounts for the creative genius and extraordinary versatility of the third president.

220

Brodie, Fawn McKay.

Thomas Jefferson, an intimate history / [by] Fawn M. Brodie. — [1st ed.]. — New York : Norton, [1974]. — 591 p. : ill.

E332 .B787

Bibliography: p. 555–565.

A psychohistory emphasizing a spurious liaison between Jefferson and Sally Hemings. Items 221 and 222 are examples of the response to this controversial assertion.

221

Miller, John Chester.

The wolf by the ears : Thomas Jefferson and slavery / John Chester Miller. — New York : Free Press, c1977. — xii, 319 p., [4] leaves of plates : ill.

E332.2 .M54

Bibliography: p. 298–307.

Examines thoroughly the paradox of slavery and Jefferson's difficulty in resolving this uniquely American problem. Miller discredits the James Callender, Fawn Brodie, and Page Smith hypotheses about the relationship between Jefferson and Sally Hemings.

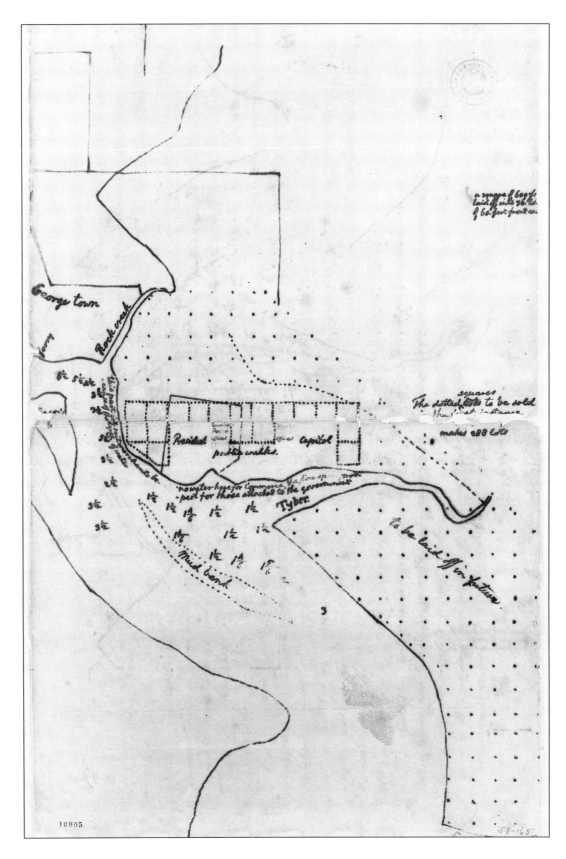

FIGURE 19. Jefferson's plan for the Federal City, ca. 1791, Original in the
Thomas Jefferson Papers, Manuscript Division, Library of Congress. (LCMS–27748–215)

222
Dabney, Virginius.
The Jefferson scandals : a rebuttal / by Virginius Dabney. — New York : Dodd, Mead, c1981. — x, 154 p. : ill.

E332.2 .D3

Bibliography: p. 143–147.

Refutes the arguments of writers, particularly Fawn Brodie, who have tried to prove a liaison between Thomas Jefferson and Sally Hemings. The author uses both original documents and printed sources, contemporary and modern, to prove his point.

223
McLaughlin, Jack.
Jefferson and Monticello : the biography of a builder / Jack McLaughlin. — 1st ed. — New York : H. Holt, c1988. — viii, 481 p. : ill.

E332.2 .M43 1988

Bibliographical references included in "Notes" (p. 391–457).

Maintains that the personal and private Jefferson is revealed via a close examination of the long construction process of Monticello. The author believes that "Those who construct their own shelter replicate themselves, at their deepest and most significant level, in their houses."

MAN OF CULTURE

Art and Architecture

224
Jefferson, Thomas.
Thomas Jefferson, architect : original designs in the collection of Thomas Jefferson Coolidge, junior / with an essay and notes, by Fiske Kimball. — Boston : Printed for private distribution at the Riverside Press, Cambridge, 1916. — vii, 205 p., l leaf, xi p., l leaf : 233 facsim (incl. front., plans) on 50 leaves, tab. diagr.

E332 .J48 Rare Bk. Coll.

Reprinted in New York with a new introd. by F.D. Nichols by Da Capo Press in 1968.

Reproduces over two hundred drawings from the Coolidge Collection housed at the Massachusetts Historical Society. Documents and drawings that have been discovered since Kimball's original research are found in Frederick Doveton Nichol's *Architectural Drawings* (1961).

225
Cripe, Helen.
Thomas Jefferson and music. — Charlottesville : University Press of Virginia, [1974]. — viii, 157 p. : ill., facsims.

ML429.J43 C7

Bibliography: p. [135]–152.

"Jefferson's Catalogue of 1783; Transcription of the Music Section": p. 97–104.

"Collections of Jefferson Family Music": p. 105–128.

226
The Eye of Th. Jefferson : [exhibition] / William Howard Adams, editor. — Washington : National Gallery of Art, 1976. — xli, 411 p. : ill. (some col.).

E332.2 .E88

Bibliography: p. 401–403.

Mounted for the Bicentennial of the American Revolution, this extensive exhibit recreates the world known to Thomas Jefferson. The exhaustive catalog describes the visual arts, as well as furniture, decorative objects, and scientific instruments from the period.

227
Jefferson and the arts : an extended view / edited and with introductions by William Howard Adams. — Washington : National Gallery of Art, 1976. — 293 p. : ill.

E332.2 .J46

Includes bibliographical references.

A companion volume to *The Eye of Th. Jefferson* (no. 226).

Contents: The life portraits of Thomas Jefferson / A. L. Bush — Jefferson as art collector / H. E. Dickson — Jefferson and Adams' English garden tour / E. Dumbauld — Jefferson, the making of an architect / F. D. Nichols — Thomas Jefferson and the planning of the National Capitol / P. F. Norton — A peep into Elysium / G. G. Shackelford — Jefferson and French eighteenth-century furniture / Sir F. Watson.

228
Rice, Howard Crosby.
Thomas Jefferson's Paris / by Howard C. Rice, Jr. — Princeton, N.J. : Princeton University Press, 1976. — ix, 156 p. : ill.

DC707 .R52

Includes bibliographical references and index.

Drawing information from Jefferson's personal papers and contemporary maps and prints, Rice recreates the Paris of 1784–1789 when Jefferson served as American minister to France. The catalog, *The Eye of Th. Jefferson*, complements this work to give a detailed view of French urban life under Louis XVI.

229
Nichols, Frederick Doveton.
Thomas Jefferson, landscape architect / Frederick Doveton Nichols and Ralph E. Griswold. — Charlottesville : University Press of Virginia, 1978. — xvii, 196 p. : ill. — (Monticello monograph series)

E332.2 .N53

Bibliography: p. [181]–188.

Establishes Jefferson as a talented and proficient landscape architect before this fine art was clearly established in America. The authors survey his designs for Richmond, Washington, D.C., Monticello and other plantations, plus his residence in Paris, enriching the text with extensive illustrations.

230
Stewart, Alva W.
Thomas Jefferson : his architectural contributions to Monticello and the University of Virginia / Alva W. Stewart and Susan J. Stewart. — Monticello, Ill. : Vance Bibliographies, [1984]. — 12 p. — (Architecture series—bibliography ; A–1210)

Z8452 .S74 1984

Lists books, theses, and journal articles from 1888 to 1981 written about Jefferson and architecture. The editors place emphasis on the structural design of the buildings rather than on landscape architecture.

Science, Education, and Religion

231
Honeywell, Roy John.
The educational work of Thomas Jefferson / by Roy J. Honeywell. — Cambridge : Harvard University Press, 1931. — xvi p., 1 leaf, 295 p. : front. (port.) plates. — (Harvard studies in education ; v. 16)

E332 .H77

Reprinted in New York by Russell & Russell in 1964.
Bibliography: p. 289–295.

Believing in education for personal fulfillment and in an educated citizenry to maintain democracy, Jefferson regarded the founding of the University of Virginia as one of his greatest and lasting achievements. Honeywell traces the development of these ideas, giving particular attention to the sources of Jefferson's views and providing illustrative documents in the appendices.

232
Healey, Robert M.
Jefferson on religion in public education. — New Haven : Yale University Press, 1962. — xi, 294 p. — (Yale publications in religion ; 3)

LC111 .H4

"A dissertation presented for the degree of doctor of philosophy at Yale University . . . somewhat revised."
Bibliography: p. [277]–284.
Reprinted in Hamden, Conn. by Archon Books in 1970.
Probes the evolution of Jefferson's religious beliefs and ties these ideas to the founder of the University of Virginia's concept of public education.

233
Benson, C. Randolph.
Thomas Jefferson as social scientist / [by] C. Randolph Benson. — Rutherford, N.J. : Fairleigh Dickinson University Press, [1971]. — 333 p.

E332.2 .B4

Bibliography: p. 313–323.
Using the methods and jargon of a sociologist, the author analyzes his subject's writings and concludes that Jefferson, a child of the Enlightenment, was the predecessor to modern social scientists.

234
Jackson, Donald Dean.
Thomas Jefferson & the Stony Mountains : exploring the West from Monticello / Donald Jackson. — Urbana : University of Illinois Press, c1981. — xii, 339 p. : maps.

E332.2 .J32

Bibliography: p. 311–324.
Centers on Jefferson's life-long interest, both scientific and political, in the Trans-Mississippi West. This study discusses the effect of the Louisiana Purchase and the Lewis and Clark Expedition on future westward expansion.

235
Bedini, Silvio A.
Thomas Jefferson and his copying machines / Silvio A. Bedini. — Charlottesville : University Press of Virginia, 1984. — xvi, 239 p. : ill. — (Monticello monograph series)

Z48 .B44 1984

Bibliography: p. 211–229.
Preserving the written word stimulated the development of mechanical copying devices in the early nineteenth century. The author organizes the evolution of the polygraph and like inventions around Jefferson's need for multiple copies and his experimentation with machines for this purpose.

236
Greene, John C.
American science in the age of Jefferson / John C. Greene. — 1st ed. — Ames : Iowa State University Press, 1984. — xiv, 484 p., [2] leaves of plates : ill. (some col.).

Q127.U6 G69 1984

Includes bibliographical references and index.
This narrative study of the period 1780–1820 focuses on American scientific development and Jefferson's importance as a promoter and practitioner of the study of natural history. The author emphasizes the religious and social forces that influenced scientists of the early national period.

237
Sanford, Charles B.
The religious life of Thomas Jefferson / Charles B. Sanford. — Charlottesville : University Press of Virginia, 1984. — 246 p

E332.2 .S255 1984

Bibliography: p. 231–234.
Selecting from a wide range of documentation, the author brings together Jefferson's thoughts and writings on religion, emphasizing objectivity and comprehensiveness rather than a new theme. An appendix lists the New Testament sources that form the compilation known as "Jefferson's Bible."

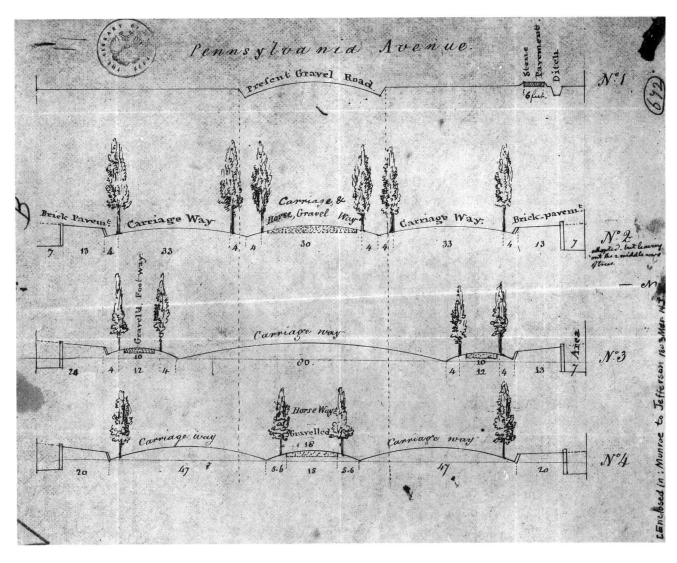

FIGURE 20.   Poplars along Pennsylvania Avenue, Design Attributed to Jefferson, 1803, Original in the Thomas Jefferson Papers, Manuscript Division, Library of Congress.   (LC–USZ62–49874)

FIGURE 21. Life Portrait Painted by Charles William Peale, December 1791. (LC–USZ62–2155)

238
Bedini, Silvio A.

Thomas Jefferson and American vertebrate paleontology / Silvio A. Bedini. — Charlottesville, Va. : Commonwealth of Va., Dept. of Mines, Minerals and Energy, Division of Mineral Resources, 1985. — 26 p. : ill. — (Virginia Division of Mineral Resources publication ; 61)
QE841 .B385 1985
Bibliography: p. 24–26.

Discusses the collecting and preserving of North American fossils in the late eighteenth century within the context of Jefferson's influence on this new science. Jefferson's active promotion of science and sponsorship of the American Philosophical Society were more important to the development of American scientific development than his actual writings on the subject.

239
Miller, Charles A. (Charles Allen)

Jefferson and nature : an interpretation / Charles A. Miller. — Baltimore : Johns Hopkins University Press, c1988. — xii, 300 p. : ill.
E332.2 .M53 1988
Bibliography: p. 283–290.

Examines Jefferson's linguistic use and philosophical understanding of nature. The author discusses the meaning of nature during the Enlightenment period and how Jefferson became the chief proponent of the concept in America.

240

Jefferson and wine : model of moderation / edited by R. De Treville Lawrence III. 2nd ed. rev. and enl. — The Plains, Va. : Vinifera Wine Growers Association, c1989. — 386 p. : ill.
TP557 .J43 1989

Reflects Jefferson's interest in wine, both as a connoisseur and as a viticulturist. The text is supplemented with personal accounts and correspondence.

MAN OF LAW AND POLITICS

241
Koch, Adrienne.

Jefferson and Madison : the great collaboration. — [1st ed.]. — New York : Knopf, 1950. — xv, 294, xiv p.
E332 .K58 1950
Bibliographical footnotes.
Reprinted in Lanham, Md., by University Press of America in 1986 (E332.2 .K63 1986).

Studies the fifty-year relationship between these fellow Virginians whose thinking, separately and together, had a profound effect on American democratic principles.

242
Cunningham, Noble E.

The Jeffersonian Republicans in power : party operations, 1801–1809. — Chapel Hill : Published for the Institute of Early American History and Culture at Williamsburg, Va., by the University of North Carolina Press, [1963]. — ix, 318 p. : facsims.
JK2316 .C82
"Bibliographical Note": p. [306]–310.
Bibliographical footnotes.

Continuing his earlier study of Jefferson's political party, *Jefferson's Republicans: The Formation of Party Organization, 1789–1801*, Cunningham focuses here on the structure and function of the party at the national and state levels. He further demonstrates how the press and patronage were necessary for effective party machinery.

243
Levy, Leonard Williams.

Jefferson & civil liberties : the darker side / Leonard W. Levy. — Cambridge : Belknap Press of Harvard University Press, 1963. — xv, 225 p.
JC599.U5 L45
Bibliography: p. 179–186.
Reprinted in Chicago by I.R. Dee in 1989.

Although Americans regard Jefferson as the author and defender of individual rights, Levy argues that the third president often violated the principles of civil liberty. He gathers evidence from Jefferson's administrations, contending that perceived threats to the republic and the absence of a workable philosophy of liberty caused Jefferson occasionally to act as an antilibertarian.

244
Kaplan, Lawrence S.

Jefferson and France : an essay on politics and political ideas / by Lawrence S. Kaplan. — New Haven : Yale University Press, 1967. — ix, 175 p.
E332.45 .K3
"Bibliographical note": p. [153]–168.
Reprinted in Westport, Conn., by Greenwood Press in 1980.

Maintains that Jefferson's political philosophy was fully developed before he went to France in 1784. Kaplan observes that the seemingly Francophile policies of the third administration were based more on a concern for a balance to British power than on a personal bias toward France.

245

Sheehan, Bernard W.

Seeds of extinction : Jeffersonian philanthropy and the American Indian. — Chapel Hill : Published for the Institute of Early American History and Culture at Williamsburg, Va., by the University of North Carolina Press, [1973]. — xii, 301 p.

E93 .S54

Bibliography: p. [281]–292.

Distinguishes clearly between Jefferson's philanthropic ideals for the Indians of North America and the practical application of this policy. Sheehan points out that the westward removal of tribes did not protect or insulate them from white civilization, but rather led directly to the disruption of tribal structure and the disintegration of their culture.

246

Sisson, Dan.

The American Revolution of 1800 / with an introd. by Harvey Wheeler. — [1st ed.]. — New York : Knopf ; [distributed by Random House], 1974. — xvii, 468, vi p.

E310 .S57 1974

Includes bibliographical references.

Based on a fresh examination of primary sources, the author contends that the American Revolution of 1776 ends, not with the Treaty of Paris in 1783, but with the election of 1800 and the peaceful transfer of power from John Adams and the Federalists to Thomas Jefferson and the Republicans.

247

Dargo, George.

Jefferson's Louisiana : politics and the clash of legal tradition / George Dargo. — Cambridge, Mass. : Harvard University Press, 1975. — x, 260 p. — (Studies in legal history)

KFL78 .D28

Based on the author's thesis, Columbia University.

Bibliography: p. [241]–251.

Analyzes the effectiveness of Jefferson's policy to supplant continental civil law with English common law in Orleans territory after the Louisiana Purchase of 1803. Both cultural differences and political events, contends Dargo, cooperated in the establishment of the Louisiana civil law digest of 1808.

248

DeConde, Alexander.

This affair of Louisiana / by Alexander DeConde. — New York : Scribner, c1976. — x, 325 p., [6] leaves of plates : ill.

E333 .D42

Bibliography: p. 279–314.

Argues that the Louisiana Purchase of 1803 was the culminating event of the expansionist policy of the early republic. DeConde uses imperialism and expansion interchangeably to demonstrate that American territorial growth continued the British imperial tradition of the colonial period.

249

McDonald, Forrest.

The presidency of Thomas Jefferson / by Forrest McDonald. — Lawrence : University Press of Kansas, c1976. — xi, 201 p., [1] leaf of plates : port. — (American presidency series)

E331 .M32

Bibliography: p. 177–191.

Continues a series that comprehensively studies the various presidential administrations. Tracing Jefferson's politics from Henry St. John, First Viscount Bolingbroke, and the English Oppositionists, McDonald explains the practical application of these ideas between 1801 and 1809 and Jefferson's success as chief executive.

250

Banning, Lance.

The Jeffersonian persuasion : evolution of a party ideology / Lance Banning. — Ithaca, N.Y. : Cornell University Press, 1978. — 307 p.

E302.1 .B2

Bibliographical footnotes.

Outlines the evolution of Jefferson's Republican party from its opposition to Federalist policies in 1789 to the dominant party after the election of 1800. Both the British origins of opposition politics and the political philosophies of the early republic are carefully detailed by Banning, who seeks to trace this development through ideas rather than events.

251

Cunningham, Noble E.

The process of government under Jefferson / by Noble E. Cunningham, Jr. — Princeton, N.J. : Princeton University Press, c1978. — xii, 357 p.

JK180 .C86

Bibliography: p. [333]–337.

Concentrates exclusively on the operation of government under Jefferson, rather than on events or personalities. The author examines not only the executive and legislative branches, but scrutinizes internal levels of government such as departmental clerks, presidential staff, and congressional committees in order to determine how they functioned between 1801 and 1808. Numerous tables and an extensive bibliographic note give evidence to the use of new material in studying governmental process.

252

Dumbauld, Edward.

Thomas Jefferson and the law / by Edward Dumbauld. — 1st ed. — Norman : University of Oklahoma Press, c1978. — xv, 293 p. : ports.

KF363.J4 D8 1978

Bibliography: p. 253–284.

Surveys Jefferson's participation in the broad realm of the legal profession. Dumbauld's work focuses on Jefferson's early legal training and law practice, as well as on his nonofficial writings about the law, particularly the Burr conspiracy trial and the Edward Livingston lawsuit involving the New Orleans Batture.

253

Johnstone, Robert M.

Jefferson and the presidency : leadership in the young Republic / Robert M. Johnstone, Jr. — Ithaca : Cornell University Press, 1978. — 332 p.

E331 .J69

Bibliography: p. [315]–326.

Evaluates the effectiveness of Jefferson as the chief executive. The revolution of 1800 was not only the peaceful transfer of power between opposing political parties, but also, Johnstone maintains, a total change in the leadership capabilities of the president. The author documents Jefferson's exceptional ability to use persuasion and cultivation of influence to bridge the distance between the executive and legislative branches of government.

254

Stuart, Reginald C.

The half-way pacifist : Thomas Jefferson's view of war / Reginald C. Stuart. — Toronto ; Buffalo : University of Toronto Press, c1978. — x, 93 p.

E332.2 .S87

Bibliography: p. [85]–90.

Extracts selections from Jefferson's writings and political actions which illustrate the often contradictory views about war held by an enlightened republican. Stuart concludes that Jefferson ultimately believed that war, although repugnant, could be necessary to preserve a nation's independence and self-determination.

255

Wills, Garry.

Inventing America : Jefferson's Declaration of Independence / Garry Wills. — 1st ed. — Garden City, N.Y. : Doubleday, 1978. — xxvi, 398 p.

E221 .W64

Includes bibliographical references and indexes.

"The Declarations of Jefferson and of the Congress": p. [374]–379.

Contrasts and compares Jefferson's draft of the Declaration with the document signed by the Continental Congress in 1776. Wills enlarges the study to include the changing viewpoints of the Declaration during the nineteenth and early twentieth centuries. He refutes the work in John Hazelton's *The Declaration of Independence* (1906) and Carl Becker's *The Declaration of Independence: A Study in the History of Political Ideas* (1922) and develops a revisionist interpretation of Jefferson's document.

256

Spivak, Burton.

Jefferson's English crisis : commerce, embargo, and the republican revolution / Burton Spivak. — Charlottesville : University Press of Virginia, 1979. — xiii, 250 p.

E331 .S68

Bibliography: p. [229]–241.

Focuses on Jefferson's foreign policy with Great Britain from 1803 to 1809. Using the embargo as an example, Spivak delineates the tension between the republican ideology of the third administration and the commercial goals of the early republic.

257

McCoy, Drew R.

The elusive Republic : political economy in Jeffersonian America / by Drew R. McCoy. — Chapel Hill : Published for the Institute of Early American History and Culture, Williamsburg, Va., by the University of North Carolina Press, c1980. — ix, 268 p.

HC105 .M235

Includes bibliographical references and index.

Emphasizes the intellectual origins of the policies of Franklin, Jefferson, and Madison in formulating their concept of a republican political economy. McCoy seeks to broaden the modern understanding of the difficulties, practical and ideological, of creating both a new system of government and a firm economic foundation for the early republic.

258

Matthews, Richard K.

The radical politics of Thomas Jefferson : a revisionist view / Richard K. Matthews. — Lawrence : University Press of Kansas, c1984. — ix, 171 p.

E332.2 .M37 1984

Bibliography: p. 157–165.

Advocates the idea that participatory democracy was the basis of Jefferson's political and economic theories. Matthews writes that the thought process underlying these theories is more important to American society than any specific structure Jefferson may have created for the United States.

259

Dewey, Frank L.

Thomas Jefferson, lawyer / Frank L. Dewey. — Charlottesville : University Press of Virginia, 1986. — xvi, 184 p.

KF363.J4 D48 1986

Notes: p. 114–167.

Bibliography: p. [168]–175.

Studies the legal career (1767–1774) of Jefferson within the cultural milieu of mid eighteenth-century Virginia. Following a general discussion of his law practice and three specific cases, the author reasons that Jefferson ended his legal practice because of frustration with the cumbersome legal process and nonpaying clients.

260

Crackel, Theodore J.

Mr. Jefferson's army : political and social reform of the military establishment, 1801–1809 / Theodore J. Crackel. — New York : New York University Press, 1987. — xiii, 250 p. : ill. — (The American social experience series ; 6)

UA25 .C73 1987

Notes: p. 185–224 ; Bibliography: p. [225]–243.

The debate in the early national period over military policy centered on the need for a constant protective force and the American opposition to a standing army. Crackel believes Jefferson resolved the impasse with the creation of a military academy at West Point that would train and maintain a professional officer corps.

261
Kaplan, Lawrence S.
   Entangling alliances with none : American foreign policy in the age of Jefferson / Lawrence S. Kaplan. — Kent, Ohio : Kent State University Press, c1987. — xvii, 230 p.
                                             E310.7 .K37 1987
Bibliography: p. [201]–223.
   Asserts that Thomas Jefferson contributed more to the development of American foreign policy from 1776 to 1820 than any other statesman. This collection of fourteen essays, thirteen of which have been published previously, is drawn together by the concluding essay on recent historiographical trends.

262
Caldwell, Lynton Keith.
   The administrative theories of Hamilton & Jefferson : their contribution to thought on public administration / Lynton K. Caldwell. — 2nd ed. — New York : Holmes & Meier, c1988. — xxiii, 244 p.
                                             JK171.A1 C3 1988
Includes bibliographical references and index.
   First published in Chicago by University of Chicago Press in 1944.
   Although both believed fundamentally in a republican form of government, Hamilton and Jefferson differed in their opinions of the administration of that government as outlined in the Constitution. In contrasting and comparing their theories, the author describes the two positions and the strong personality influences of each man. Caldwell concludes his work with an analysis of their conflicts and contributions to the present structure of the U.S. government.

FAMILY, HOMES, AND HAUNTS

(Entries are arranged chronologically by date of publication.)

263
Randolph, Sarah N. (Sarah Nicholas)
   The domestic life of Thomas Jefferson. — New York : Harper & brothers, 1871. — xiii p., 1 leaf, [17]–432 p. : ill., front., plates, ports., plan, facsims.
                                             E332.25 .R2 1871
Reprinted in Charlottesville for the Thomas Jefferson Memorial Foundation by the University Press of Virginia in 1978.
   Drawing on her childhood at Monticello and her memories of her great-grandfather, the author recalls the private side of a public family. Although the letters are included in the numerous editions of Jefferson's papers, the work's unique quality derives from the anecdotes and personal comments of Jefferson family members.

264
Jefferson, Thomas.
   To the girls and boys : being the delightful little-known letters of Thomas Jefferson to and from his children and grandchildren. — New York : Funk & Wagnalls, [1964]. — x, 210 p. : ill., facsims., geneal. table (on lining papers), ports.
                                             E332 .86 1964
This selection of letters between Jefferson, his daughters, Martha and Mary, and five of Martha's children clearly shows the love and concern he felt for his progeny. It depicts a dimension not evident to those outside the family circle.

265
Jefferson, Thomas.
   The family letters of Thomas Jefferson / edited by Edwin Morris Betts and James Adam Bear, Jr. — Columbia : University of Missouri Press, [1966]. — 506 p. : ill., geneal. table, maps, ports.
                                             E332 .86 1966
Reprinted in Charlottesville for the Thomas Jefferson Memorial Foundation by the University Press of Virginia in 1986.
   Brings together 570 letters, dated 1783–1826, written either to or from Jefferson, his daughters, and their children. This annotated compilation clarifies the varying personal names and relationships of the three generations of this close-knit family.

266
Adams, William Howard.
   Jefferson's Monticello / by William Howard Adams ; with principal photography by Langdon Clay. — 1st ed. — New York : Abbeville Press, c1983. — x, 276 p. : ill. (some col.).
                                             E332.74 .A3 1983
Bibliography: p. 269–271.
   Comprehensively traces the history and development of Jefferson's "unsurpassed autobiographical legacy" from the earliest drawing of 1767 to the present. Adams's text is extensively complemented by drawings and photographs. The epilogue, documenting the fate of Monticello after Jefferson's death in 1826, provides a glimpse of opposing decorating styles: classical architecture vs. Victorian furnishings.

267

Llewellyn, Robert.

Thomas Jefferson's Monticello / foreword by Dumas Malone ; photography by Robert Llewellyn ; commentary by Charles Granquist. — Charlottesville, Va. : Thomasson-Grant, 1983. — 112 p. : col. ill.

E332.74 .L58 1983

An artistic photo essay depicting the changing moods of the house from dawn until dusk.

268

Betts, Edwin Morris.

Thomas Jefferson's flower garden at Monticello / Edwin Morris Betts and Hazlehurst Bolton Perkins. — 3rd ed. revised and enlarged by Peter J. Hatch. — Charlottesville : published for the Thomas Jefferson Memorial Foundation, Inc. by the University Press of Virginia, 1986. — ix, 96 p., [16] p. of plates : ill. (some col.).

E332.74 .B48 1986

Bibliography: p. [95]–96.

Describes the flowers and the planting sequence originally conceived for Monticello. Species new to Virginia and the United States were chosen by Jefferson over the typical plantings of the period. A diagram of the restored gardens and an annotated list of the individual flowers complete the work.

269

Langhorne, Elizabeth Coles.

Monticello, a family story / Elizabeth Langhorne. — Chapel Hill, N.C. : Algonquin Books of Chapel Hill, 1987. — xi, 289 p., [24] p. of plates : ill.

E332.74 .L36 1987

"Bibliographic Notes": p. 271–285.

Concentrates on the Jefferson family and the strain that long public service placed on personal relationships. Langhorne uses the observations of Jefferson's children and grandchildren to create a picture of private life at Monticello.

NAME AND TITLE INDEX

(Numbers refer to entries, not pages.)

ISBN 0-16-041610-8